ROUGH GUIDES

POCKET **ROUGH GUIDE**
ISLE OF SKYE
& THE WESTERN ISLES

written and researched by
PAUL STAFFORD
this edition updated by
JOANNA REEVES

CONTENTS

ISLE OF SKYE & THE WESTERN ISLES

Gaelic culture and history reigns supreme in the wild, remote northwest fringes of Scotland. The 130-mile-long archipelago known as the Western Isles is Scotland's rocky breakwater, taking a battering from the North Atlantic. Skye, meanwhile, is no sheltered isle either, with its remarkable rock formations sculpted by the elements over millions of years. Yet these sparsely populated lands have an uncanny knack of bringing people back for more. Perhaps it's the pristine white-sand beaches, the feeling of heading off the beaten trail in an otherwise well-connected country, or the kind of hospitality (and soul-nourishing seafood chowder) that warms even the chilliest of days, but there's a unique splendour to Skye and the Western Isles that can tame the wildest heart.

Liniclate Beach on Benbecula

Many visitors are quick to recognize the great contrast between Skye and the remoter Western Isles (also known as the Outer Hebrides). While the Skye Bridge links its namesake to the mainland, the Western Isles are cast adrift in the unforgiving North Atlantic Ocean. Ferries and flights provide the only means of public access, and when the weather is poor, as it frequently is, they are effectively forced into isolation. Skye feels more urbane, with the majority of the population living in small towns, after the Clearances emptied the crofts, which soon fell into disuse. Crofting remains very much a way of life, though, in the wilder Western Isles. Here, on the edge of the world, the islands' interiors can seem remote and almost lunar, although the coastal areas have more of a rugged lived-in feel to them, despite the oft-unfavourable climate.

There is so much to see and do in Skye and the Western Isles that you could spend weeks unlocking one region after the next, but even if you only have a few days available, it's still possible to get a real sense of what life on the islands is all about. The geological oddities of the Trotternish peninsula, the towering Cuillin mountains and

It's sheep, not traffic, that tends to clog up the streets in the Western Isles

the prehistoric Callanish Standing Stones are all accessible on a day-trip from the main cities on their respective islands. Many of the more secluded highlights, however, would be difficult to reach without your own vehicle, or indeed via an organized boat trip in the case of the smaller islands. It usually takes much longer than you'd expect to get around the archipelago, and attempts to see all the major sights in a day are discouraged by the local tourism authority.

When to visit

Unpredictable, in a word, sums up the weather in this region of Scotland. The best conditions for travel here usually occur in April, May, September and early October, when the temperature is mild, the skies less tempestuous, and nature is at its most resplendent. Summer months coincide with the high season, but worse still, the midge season as well. Clouds of the tiny biting insects can turn lovely, calm weather into a misery. At any point of the year in the Western Isles, it can feel like you've experienced all four seasons in one day. Reduced opening hours are common throughout the winter. Public transport, including flights and ferries, operate on a reduced timetable during this period. Many of the boat trips cease entirely. In winter, days have been known for their crisp, bright weather, but snow and rain are more common. Nevertheless, some people still venture this way in winter and are usually rewarded by having major sights to themselves and, further north, the chance to witness the majesty of the aurora borealis.

Sunrise over the Quiraing on the Isle of Skye

Travelling by car is recommended unless you have the time, energy and inclination to cover the distances under your own steam. While the A87, Skye's main road, is frequently rendered gridlocked in the summer months, the Western Isles are strung together by an ambitious assortment of often empty roads and ferries. They traverse a wild landscape blighted by lochs, tapering off to a lonely point at Vatersay in the south. Wherever you are in this region, all you have to do is veer off the tourist trail and you'll be greeted by serene montane panoramas, ancient ruins and beguiling coastlines.

Whatever your schedule and budget, be sure to sample the region's excellent cuisine. From a simple fish and chips supper perched on a bench overlooking a loch, to a decadent seafood feast at a Michelin-starred restaurant, the Outer Hebrides has an exciting culinary scene. Skye, in particular, has emerged as a foodie destination. An ever-growing crop of distilleries is cropping up across the islands: Skye, North Uist, Raasay and Lewis and Harris all have home-grown makers concocting whiskies and, more recently, gins. Most, like the Talisker Distillery, are open to visitors on guided tours and tastings.

The archipelago is rich in Gaelic culture. Every July, the streets of Stornoway come alive with festivities for the Hebridean Celtic Festival, which competes for tourists' attention with Fèis an Eilein on the Isle of Skye. If you're travelling outside of summer, you'll find plenty of ceilidhs and live – usually impromptu – Celtic music performances enlivening the pubs all year round.

What's new

The Bracken Hide has been making waves on the hotel scene since opening on Skye in 2023. Set on the western fringes of Portree, this wilderness lodge is designed to blend into the landscape, with a stone-built main lodge and 45 wooden cabins, each with underfloor heating and mountain views, scattered across 52 acres. There's a whisky room, restaurant, sauna and wild swimming. Over on Benbecula, the North Uist Distillery is shaking things up in its new lodgings, where whisky is now brewing alongside its award-winning Downpour gins.

Where to...

Shop

Given that the largest settlement in this book (Stornoway) is home to a mere 6000 people, markets and malls don't exist in Skye and the Western Isles. However, there are plenty of local **arts and crafts** shops, particularly around Broadford and Portree on Skye. Candles, ceramics and knitwear are common examples. You can follow the **Skye Creative Trail** to visit many of the studios and see the work in progress. Lewis and Harris is known for its revered **Harris Tweed**, which mostly goes towards making durable items of clothing. Where **food and drink** are concerned, if it's a locally sourced, edible ingredient that can be distilled or wood-smoked, there's a chance you can buy it. Smoked salmon, whisky and gin all make for good souvenirs.

OUR FAVOURITES: Skyeskyns see page 32, Hebridean Smokehouse see page 89, Isle of Harris Distillery see page 76.

Drink

This is Scotland. No island village is complete without a cosy pub with a roaring fire and a good selection of drinks to help ward off the cold. **Portree** and **Stornoway** are two of the few places where you'll find more than one drinking den. In most villages, the bars are located inside a hotel that welcomes in non-guests for a tipple. In **the Western Isles** especially, you might even catch an impromptu Celtic music session, and many host ceilidh nights. As with all bars in this part of the world, on Friday and Saturday nights things can get especially boisterous.

OUR FAVOURITES: Seumas' Bar see page 49, The Criterion Bar see page 75, Am Politician see page 95.

Eat

Skye has long been the culinary capital of Scotland's northwest. Lately, however, a crop of fine restaurants has sprung up across **North Uist** and **Lewis and Harris**, putting these islands firmly on the foodie map. Locally caught **seafood** like Minch langoustine, Isle of Lewis mussels, plump scallops, peat-smoked salmon, and classics like cod and hake are all commonly found around the islands. Add to this some pan-Scottish favourites like **haggis** and **black pudding**, neeps and tatties (turnips/swede and potatoes), chased by a dram of peaty **whisky**, and you'll be sated like an islander.

OUR FAVOURITES: The Three Chimneys see page 34, Loch Bay see page 34, Uig Sands Restaurant see page 75.

Go out

You'd be hard-pressed to find a nightclub on the islands, but there are plenty of lively pubs where live music is commonplace. And if you fancy a dance, enquire locally to see if there's a **ceilidh** brewing. Skye and the Western Isles have plenty of pubs that serve great food, and a typical night out combines a good meal with a drink or two. During the summer, things liven up with music festivals.

OUR FAVOURITES: The Old Inn see page 49, Merchant Bar see page 35, Westford Inn see page 89.

Isle of Skye & the Western Isle at a glance

Flannan Isles

ATLANTIC OCEAN

Arid

Harris p.76.

Harris is renowned for its immaculate beaches, yet there are lofty mountains, historic churches and teeming flora and fauna to command the attention as well. Boats depart for distant St Kilda in the summer.

Boreray
Soay *St Kilda*
Hirta

Scarp

Taransay

Pabbay Leverbur
Berneray

North Uist p.84.

Long, empty beaches, loch-studded lunar landscapes and a scattering of mysterious prehistoric sites make North Uist one of the wildest regions of the Western Isles. People also come for the wildlife and fishing opportunities.

North Uist
Lochmadd

Monach Islands

Benbecula

Benbecula and South Uist p.90.

From machair plains to craggy mountain peaks, the beach-fringed islands of Benbecula and South Uist are peaceful and remote. Quiet crofting villages dot the rugged landscape, which still bears the scars of RAF missile testing sites.

South Uist
Beinn Mhor (2034ft)

Lochboisdale

Eriskay

Barra and Vatersay p.96.

Planes land on the beach at Barra, a dramatic arrival to an impressive island. Although small in size, you'll find many examples of the natural and man-made wonders common throughout the Western Isles here, plus a castle in a bay.

Barra
winter only
Castlebay
Vatersay
Sandray
Pabbay
Mingulay
Barra Head

Butt of Lewis
Port of Ness

Lewis p.60.
Traditional crofting villages
buffeted by North Sea winds,
prehistoric relics and the gentle
clackity-clack of Harris Tweed
looms lend a certain mystique
to Lewis. Traditional Gaelic culture
is prevalent everywhere on the island.

Barvas

Garenin
Carloway
Bernera
Callanish
Standing
Stones
Stornoway

L e w i s

H a r r i s

ham
19ft]

Tarbert

Scalpay

Shiant
Isles

**Skye: Portree, Trotternish,
Waternish and Duirinish p.24.**
Explore the geological riches of
this ultra-photogenic island, which
is dotted with castles, ancient ruins,
Gaelic heritage and gourmet
restaurants throughout.

Clement's
urch

L i t t l e   M i n c h

T h e   M i n c h

N

Uig

Trotternish

Rona

Waternish

**Skye: Minginish,
the Cuillin, Sleat
and Raasay p.36.**
Experience Skye's wilder,
less-visited side, with its
formidable mountain peaks,
plentiful wildlife, hiking
paths and distillery tours.

Neist
Point
Duirinish

Portree

Raasay

Skye

Minginish

Scalpay

The Cuillin
Broadford

Sleat

Canna

S M A L L   I S L E S

Armadale

The Small Isles p.50.
Take a boat trip out to the
perfect Hebridean islands
of Rùm, Eigg, Muck and
Canna to find ancient volcanic peaks, golden-
sand beaches, basalt cliffs
and cacophonous seabird
colonies.

Rùm

Mallaig

Hyskeir

Arisaig

Eigg

Muck

Things not to miss

It's not possible to see everything that Skye and the Western Isles have to offer in one trip, and we don't suggest you try. What follows is a selection of highlights to give you a broad taste of the region, from traditional crofts to captivating landscapes and Neolithic sites.

> **Callanish Standing Stones**
See page 70
Scotland's very own Stonehenge, this collection of Neolithic standing stones is believed to have been erected over 4600 years ago.

< **The Cuillin**
See page 39
A flurry of precipitous peaks forms Skye's impressive mountain range, twelve of which are listed as Munros.

∨ **Trotternish peninsula**
See page 25
This wild corner of Skye is sculpted by curious rock formations, heaving pinnacles and saw-toothed ridges, with dinosaur footprints adding palaeontological mystique to the geology.

< Island boat rides
See page 18
Hop aboard a boat to discover remote lochs, explore isolated islands or to go in search of wildlife, including seals, whales and dolphins.

∨ St Kilda cruise
See page 82
The westernmost archipelago of Scotland's Western Isles, and a Unesco World Heritage Site, is only accessible via an organized boat trip.

< **Eigg**
See page 53
A quintessential Hebridean island, with its own craggy hill, sandy beach, Gaelic charm and panoramic views of the neighbouring islands.

∨ **Harris beaches**
See page 78
Although frequently ranked among the finest beaches in the world, these comely stretches of sand are often deserted.

∧ Skye's gourmet scene
See pages 33 and 47
Follow the culinary trail to Skye and sample the bounty of the island's natural larder at lochside oyster shacks, traditional inns and Michelin-starred restaurants.

< Dunvegan Castle and Gardens
See page 30
Clan MacLeod's ancestral seat is a boxy fortress with well-manicured gardens, and a smattering of intriguing historical exhibits.

∧ Talisker Distillery
See page 41
Take a tour of a working whisky distillery for a behind-the-scenes glimpse of copper pot stills, oak casks and giant mash tuns, followed by a tasting or two.

∨ Harris Tweed
See page 61
See how the durable, fashionable material is made in small workshops across Lewis and Harris, and shop for souvenirs to take home with you.

∧ **Gearrannan
Blackhouse Village**
See page 69
Get a glimpse of how most people
lived on Lewis and Harris less
than a century ago in a carefully
preserved blackhouse village.

< **The Hebridean Way**
See page 97
Attempt to cycle the entire length
of the Western Isles from the tip
of Lewis to the dinky island of
Vatersay in the south.

< **Eriskay**
See page 94
With free-roaming Eriskay ponies, a string of boulder-strewn sandy beaches and a solo pub containing artefacts from a nearby shipwreck, this tiny island packs a mighty punch.

∨ **Skye Creative Trail**
See page 39
Discover a variety of arts and crafts workshops run by local artisans and get off Skye's beaten path in the process.

Three-day Skye explorer

Skye's big-hitting sights can get crowded, but combine one or two of them with a few lesser-known highlights for a more rounded view of what the island has to offer.

Armadale Castle, Gardens and Museum. See page 36. Learn all about the history of Clan Donald at their former ancestral seat in Armadale, then wander the beautifully manicured gardens.

Loch Coruisk. See page 40. Take a boat from Elgol, looking out for dolphins and seals along the way. Then spend a few hours exploring the charming Loch Coruisk.

🍴 **Lunch.** See page 49. Refuel with a plate of haggis, neaps and tatties at the cavernous *Seumas' Bar*, washed down with a local beer, before taking a little amble up Glen Sligachan.

Portree. See page 24. Stroll around the Lump and past the candy-coloured houses strung along the harbour of Skye's capital.

Skye gourmet dining. See page 34. Sample Scottish food with a French twist at the Michelin-starred *Loch Bay* restaurant (be sure to book in advance).

Neist Point Lighthouse. See page 31. Strike out along wild cliffs populated by seabirds to an exposed lighthouse poised on the cragged headland.

Talisker Distillery. See page 41. Try a peaty dram and learn how Skye's oldest legal distillery makes its revered elixir on a tour.

🍷 **Drink.** See page 35. Step inside the characterful *Stein Inn*, which hasn't changed much since opening in 1790.

Trotternish peninsula. See page 25. Dedicate your third day to the Trotternish peninsula in all its untamed geological glory.

Armadale Castle

Wildlife at Loch Coruisk

The candy-coloured houses of Portree

Three-day Western Isles-hopper

Cram into three days what cyclists do in six by driving the Hebridean Way. This frees up time to relish the historical relics and natural beauty of these enchanting islands.

Vatersay. See page 100. Linger on the remote beach at Vatersay Bay, a pristine half-mile sandy stretch backed by untamed dunes.

Barra. See page 96. Time your visit with a flight arrival to see the plane come into land on the sandy runway. Swing by the Isle of Barra Distillers to pick up a bottle of its award-winning Barra Atlantic Gin.

Lunch. See page 95. Gorge on fresh seafood in Eriskay's famed *AM Politician* pub, which took its name from the vessel that ran aground offshore in 1941 – ask to see the original whisky bottle retrieved from the foundered ship.

The sandy beach at Vatersay Bay

Neolithic North Uist. See page 85. Admire the Barpa Langass chambered burial cairn before swinging by the little-visited Pobull Fhinn standing stones, which have endured the elements for millennia.

South Harris beaches. See page 78. Sink your toes into the fine white sand on of one of the most spectacular beaches in the world.

Callanish Standing Stones. See page 70. Come up with your own theory as to the purpose of the dozens of standing stones that gaze out over the Isle of Lewis' tattered coastline.

Callanish Standing Stones

Butt of Lewis Lighthouse. See page 67. Picnic on the untamed beach beside contorted rock formations at the northern tip of the Western Isles.

Dinner. See page 73. Head into the capital of Lewis and Harris and indulge in a seafood dinner at one of a slew of gourmet restaurants cementing Stornoway's culinary reputation.

Butt of Lewis Lighthouse

Island life

Between Lewis and Harris, Skye and the Small Isles, you can soak up the unique, traditional way of life that allowed people to thrive in these remote corners of Britain.

Bullough Mausoleum. See page 52. Marvel at the Bullough Mausoleum, an extraordinary Neoclassical temple built by Sir George for his father, and all the more incongruous for its rural blackhouse-dotted surrounds.

Harris Tweed Authority. See page 62. Drop by the official authority on Harris Tweed to see a live weaving in process or to learn more about the Western Isles fashion staple.

Cleadale Crofting Museum – Eigg. See page 54. Pop in to the unmanned old blackhouse on Eigg, a reminder of harder times.

Traditional culture lives on in Harris

Lunch. See page 57. Grab a bite at a remote island eatery like *Galmisdale Bay*, where the local charm can be felt most keenly. You might even find there's a locally brewed beer on tap.

Skye Museum of Island Life. See page 28. Learn about life in the old working crofting villages of Skye before the Clearances.

Skye Creative Trail. See page 39. Discover a string of craft studios and galleries where you can watch the island's artisans at work, and perhaps pick up an authentic handmade souvenir.

Gillean beer on tap

Gearrannan Blackhouse Village. See page 69. Step back in time to when people lived in thatched homes cleverly designed to combat nuisances like midges; some of these well-preserved blackhouses serve as bunkhouses – albeit with more mod-cons than the originals.

Dinner. See page 74. Round off the day with a visit to the nautically themed *HS-1 Café Bar* for a quality fish and chips supper.

Harris tweed, a staple of the Western Isles

Wildlife and wilderness

Ultimately, what Skye and the Western Isles do best of all is nature, from wave-pounded rocks sheltering seabirds to otherworldly basalt plateaux ripe for exploration on foot.

Birdwatching on Canna. See page 55. Discover entire cliffs full of fulmars, gannets, razorbills and puffins on this remote island wildlife refuge.

Hiking the Rùm Cuillin. See page 53. Pick your way over the striking ridges of the lesser-known Cuillin range, which receive comparatively few visitors to its Skye cousin.

Skye wildlife-spotting tours. See page 40. Look to the seas for surfacing porpoises, dolphins and the occasional whale on an exhilarating boat tour.

The Cuillin. See page 39. Test your mettle on Skye's mighty mountain range, either with a guide on the challenging peaks, or through the glen to Loch Coruisk.

Lunch. See page 34. Recharge with a top-end gourmet meal at one of Skye's respected restaurants, such as *The Three Chimneys*.

St Kilda cruise. See page 82. Take a special boat tour to the distant isles of St Kilda, where the giant stacks rise up out of the water like some prehistoric bastion. Cross your fingers that the weather is good enough to dock.

Hiking in the Uists. See pages 84 and 90. Explore the barren natural environment of the Uist islands with a hike up a lonely mountain for views out over the archipelago.

Drinks. See page 101. After all that time spent in the great outdoors, warm up with a wee dram by the fire at the *Castlebay Bar* on Barra.

Hiking around the Isle of Skye

A wildlife cruise off the Isle of Harris

Puffins on Canna Island

PLACES

View over the Cuillin Hills from Sgurr na Stri

Skye: Portree, Trotternish, Waternish and Duirinish

The Isle of Skye (An t-Eilean Sgitheanach) is the Highlands in miniature. With its superb hiking routes, abundant wildlife and traditional villages, it crams much of the region's appeal into one manageable island. Yet the northern half of Skye has plenty of unique features separating it from the south: its coastline never seems to sit still, swerving and contorting into cliffs, bays and peninsulas. The landscape is at its most eccentric in this corner of the island, where inclement weather and geological processes have mangled the gneiss rock into the most enchanting of shapes. Over the past few decades, a new generation of islanders, including an influx of younger settlers, has introduced a vibrant arts and crafts scene while revolutionizing the culinary landscape. This added dose of sophistication means the island is no longer solely the preserve of hikers and coach tours. Many artisans have settled in the north and visiting their workshops is a good excuse to head off the beaten path. Even at its busiest, you're still likely to find a small pocket of Skye all to yourself.

Postcard-pretty Portree

Portree

MAP PAGE 26

Skye's capital, **Portree**, has a population of around 2500, which hardly makes it a metropolis. If anything, the town has a small-village feel and is one of the most attractive ports in northwest Scotland. Head along **Bosville Terrace** for the best views of its cliff-edged, nineteenth-century harbour filled with fishing boats and ringed by multicoloured houses.

Somerled Square

MAP PAGE 26

At the centre of town, **Somerled Square** acts as the island's main bus station, serving the rest of the island. Every Tuesday evening during the summer months, the Isle of Skye Pipe Band sets up in

Arrival and information

Intercity buses from Inverness and Glasgow arrive at and depart from Somerled Square on their way to and from Uig in the north of the island. Times and durations vary throughout the year; you can consult timetables and purchase tickets from www.citylink. co.uk. Local buses depart regularly for Broadford, Flodigarry and Uig. More information can be found online at Traveline (www. traveline.info) and Stagecoach (www.stagecoachbus.com). There is also a small car park in Somerled Square for stays of up to two hours, costing £2 from Mon–Sat. Driving is by far the best means exploring Skye and the Western Isles. Relying on public transport will limit your experience of the island to the main settlements and tourist traps.

The main VisitScotland **tourist office** for Skye is in the centre of Portree (Bayfield House, Bayfield Road; Thurs–Mon 9am–5pm, Wed 10am–5pm). The team can assist with information about local sights, booking buses elsewhere in Scotland, arranging tours, and even sourcing accommodation for those who have arrived without a booking. Hotels and restaurants are frequently fully booked in advance. Especially where accommodation is concerned, it is wise to book as far ahead as possible, even in winter, where the number of rooms available is lower due to many B&Bs and guest houses closing for the winter.

the square and puts on a bagpiping show. In winter, you may catch them practicing in the **Church of Scotland** across the road, or the *Royal Hotel* nearby.

The Lump

MAP PAGE 26

Looming behind the town is a low hill affectionately named **The Lump**, a steep and stumpy peninsula on which public hangings once attracted crowds of up to five thousand. A walkway circumvents the rocky outcrop and takes around 15 minutes to complete at a gentle amble. At the top, there's a small, dilapidated tower built in 1829, with fine views over the town.

Isle of Skye Candle Co. Visitor Centre

MAP PAGE 26
Viewfield Rd.
Pizzeria www.gastaportrigh.co.uk.
LAS cinema www.lasportrigh.co.uk.
Portree's much-loved Aros Centre changed hands in 2022, and the community cultural hub is now the **Isle of Skye Candle Co. Visitor Centre**, home to a flagship store packed with beautiful homeware items like handmade ceramics, butter-soft throws and, of course, scented candles. The candle company spent a year renovating the landmark building, retaining the original cinema and theatre but also making space for a new pizzeria and pop-up yoga and wellness studio.

Trotternish peninsula

MAP PAGE 26
Protruding twenty miles north of Portree, the **Trotternish peninsula** lays claim to some of the island's most bizarre scenery, particularly on the east coast, where volcanic basalt has pressed down on softer sandstone and limestone, causing massive landslides. These, in turn, have created sheer cliffs, peppered with outcrops of hard, wizened basalt – rocky pinnacles and pillars that are at their most eccentric in

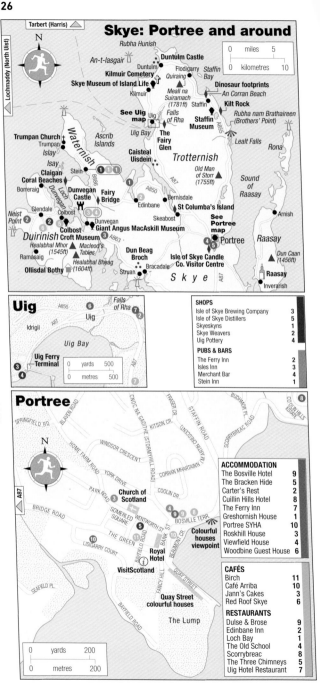

the Quiraing, above Staffin Bay, the long arc of beach unfurling just to the north of Staffin village.

Old Man of Storr

MAP PAGE 26
Bus #57A from Portree.
www.thestorr.com.

The most celebrated column of rock on Skye, the **Old Man of Storr** is all that remains after one massive landslip. Huge blocks of stone still occasionally break off the cliff of the Storr (2358ft) above. A half-hour trek from a car park ascends to the pillar, but don't expect to have it to yourself, for this is one of the island's signature sights, and will be busy whatever the weather.

Lealt Falls

MAP PAGE 26
Bus #57A from Portree

Five miles north of the Old Man of Storr, a signposted turn swerves west to the **Lealt Falls** at the head of a gorge which is largely in shadow (and home to crack squadrons of midges in summer). The views across to Raasay and Rona from the first stage of the path are spectacular on clear days. A **viewing platform** opened in 2019 to make the most of these scenic surrounds. The coast here is worth exploring, too, especially the track leading to **Rubha nam Brathairean** (Brothers' Point).

Kilt Rock

MAP PAGE 26
Bus #57A from Portree

With spectacular tubular, basalt columns that plummet into the sea – like the folds in a kilt, apparently – and cliffs dotted with fulmar and kittiwake, it's little surprise **Kilt Rock** is a popular call on the tourist route. An impressive waterfall that cascades 170ft down the rockface only adds to the natural drama. The car park is located a few miles north of the Lealt Falls turn.

Staffin Museum

MAP PAGE 26
Elishader, Staffin, Bus #57A from Portree.
www.staffindinosaurmuseum.com. Charge.

Things start to get a little more prehistoric at **Staffin Museum**. The modest collection contains some intriguing local finds, including a selection of dinosaur bones, Neolithic arrow heads and information about Skye's dinosaur footprints. If you plan to visit An Corran Beach, check in here first to find out the day's low tide hours – the only time the dinosaur footprints are visible. Tours are also available, as the footprints are tricky to locate.

An Corran Beach

MAP PAGE 26
Bus #57A from Portree

A family of dinosaurs walked along **An Corran Beach** some 165 million years ago. The evidence of their passing has been etched into the rocks ever since. These remarkable Jurassic relics are covered by the high tide and often by sand or seaweed at low tide. They are, needless to say, difficult to locate, but there are information boards nearby to help guide you. Follow Staffin Road to the Harbour

A 170ft-high waterfall spills over Kilt Rock

Duntulm Castle

car park. From there, it's possible to pick your way back over the rocks to the remarkably preserved tracks.

Quiraing

MAP PAGE 26

Just past Staffin Bay, a single-track road cuts east across the peninsula into the **Quiraing**, a spectacular area contoured by jagged pinnacles, sheer cliffs and curious rock formations produced by landslip over millions of years. The ever-shifting landscape is still geologically active and moves a few centimetres every year. There are two car parks: from the first, beside a cemetery, it's a steep half-hour climb to the rocks; from the second, on the saddle, it's a longer but gentler traverse. Once you're among the rocks, you can make out "The Prison" to your right, and the 131ft "Needle" to your left. "The Table", a sunken platform where locals used to play shinty, lies a further fifteen-minute scramble up the rocks.

Duntulm

MAP PAGE 26

Bus #57C from Portree

Beyond Flodigarry, four miles further along the A855, lies

Duntulm (Duntuilm), whose heyday as a MacDonald power base is recalled by the shattered remains of a dilapidated but impressively perched headland fortress abandoned by the clan in 1732; they say a clumsy nurse dropped the baby son and heir from a window onto the rocks below. They also say you can see the keel marks of Viking longships scoured into the rocks.

Skye Museum of Island Life

MAP PAGE 26

On the A855, 2 miles southwest of Duntulm. Bus #57C from Portree. www.skyemuseum.co.uk. Charge.

It's a short trip from Duntulm to the best of the island's folk museums. Run by a local family, the **Skye Museum of Island Life** – an impressive collection of eight thatched blackhouses decorated with home furnishings and farming tools – provides an insight into a way of life commonplace only a century ago. Behind the museum is **Kilmuir Cemetery**, which contains the graves of Flora MacDonald, heroine during Bonnie Prince Charlie's flight, and her husband. Such was her fame that the original mausoleum fell victim to souvenir hunters and had to be replaced. The Celtic cross headstone is inscribed with a tribute by Dr Johnson, who visited her in 1773: "Her name will be mentioned in history, if courage and fidelity be virtues mentioned with honour."

Uig

MAP PAGE 26

Bus #57C from Portree

Skye's chief ferry port for the Western Isles is **Uig** (Uige; pronounced "oo-ig"), which curves its way round a dramatic horseshoe bay. CalMac Ferries leave from here for Lochmaddy in North Uist and Tarbert in Harris. The village is mostly quiet, with Skye Brewing Co. beside the harbour and a short walk inland along the small stream to the pretty **Falls of Rha**.

The Fairy Glen

MAP PAGE 26

Strike out on the lovely, gentle walk up **The Fairy Glen** (officially known as Glen Uig) to wander through a Hobbity landscape of miniature hills centred around a single basalt outcrop that looks like a ruin. Sadly, in Skye anything with the word 'fairy' in the name has become inordinately popular with tourists, which in turn has led to all-too-frequent disrespectful behaviour. One example is the creation of stone spirals by pulling rocks from their natural place, which locals are then forced to repeatedly dismantle to maintain the original state of the glen.

St Columba's Island

MAP PAGE 26

Bus #56 from Portree

A fascinating medieval burial ground graces a small islet in the middle of River Snizort. Located near the village of Skeabost along the A850, **St Columba's Island** once hosted a church from 1079–1498, and 28 chiefs of the Nicolson clan have been buried here; some beneath remarkable gravestones scored with relief carvings of warriors and various symbols.

Waternish peninsula

MAP PAGE 26

Waternish is a backwater by Skye's standards. Though not as spectacular as Duirinish or Trotternish, it provides equally good views over to the Western Isles and, with fewer visitors, feels appealingly remote. To reach the peninsula, cross the **Fairy Bridge** (Beul-Ath nan Tri Allt or "Ford of the Three Burns") at the junction of the B886. Legend has it that the fourth MacLeod clan chief was forced to say farewell to his fairy wife here when she had to return to her kind. Her parting gift was the Fairy Flag (see page 30).

Stein

MAP PAGE 26

Stein, looking out over Loch Bay to the Western Isles, is Waternish's prettiest village: a string of whitewashed cottages built in 1787 by the British Fisheries Society. The place never really took off and was more or less abandoned within a couple of generations. Today, it's a little livelier, thanks to Michelin-starred *Loch Bay*, its world-class restaurant helmed by chef-owner Michael Smith, and the historic *Stein Inn* – a locals' favourite since 1790. There are few nicer places on Skye for a leisurely pint on a sunny summer evening.

Trumpan Church

MAP PAGE 26

At the end of the road that continues north from Stein is the medieval shell of **Trumpan Church**. Its beautiful location belies one of the bloodiest episodes in Skye's history. In a revenge attack in 1578, the MacDonalds of Uist set fire to the church while numerous MacLeods were attending a service within. Everyone perished except one young girl, who squeezed through a window and raised the alarm. The MacLeods rallied and slaughtered the MacDonalds, then threw their bodies into a nearby dyke. In the graveyard is the **Trial Stone**. In the fourteenth century, accused criminals were blindfolded and if they could fit their fingers in its hole, they were deemed innocent. Otherwise, ouch.

Dunvegan

MAP PAGE 26

Bus #56 from Portree

Dunvegan (Dùn Bheagain) is something of a let-down if you arrive from the south, where the west-coast route skirts the bony sea cliffs and stacks of the west coast. Yet it has one of Skye's most famous traditional sights, plus two of the island's more interesting peninsulas, Duirinish and Waternish, in its backyard. In town, the **Giant Angus MacAskill Museum** is a curious homage to the tallest Scotsman who ever lived inside a traditional thatched building. He was 7ft8in (2.36m) tall.

Dunvegan Castle and Gardens

MAP PAGE 26

1 mile north of Dunvegan, Bus #56 from Portree. www.dunvegancastle.com. Charge.

Just north of the village, **Dunvegan Castle** sprawls over a rocky outcrop, sandwiched between the sea and several acres of attractive **gardens**. It's been the seat of Clan MacLeod since the thirteenth century – and the chief still lives here with his family for part of the year – but the present facade is a product of Victorian romanticism. Older architecture remains inside, where you get the usual furniture and oil paintings alongside some more noteworthy items, with tour guides on hand to bring the history to life. The most intriguing display is the shabby remnants of the **Fairy Flag**, carried back to Skye, they say, by the Gaelic boatmen of King Harald Hardrada after the Battle of Stamford Bridge in 1066. MacLeod tradition states that the flag was the gift of a fairy to protect the clan.

As late as World War II, MacLeod pilots carried pictures of it for luck. **Seal-spotting** boat trips on Loch Dunvegan are available from the grounds during the summer.

Claigan Coral Beaches

MAP PAGE 26

Keep it quiet, but these beaches in **Claigan**, three miles north of Dunvegan, might be as good a reason to visit this area as the castle. The strands are not coral but calcified maerl (seaweed) and tiny seashells. On a sunny day, the white sands and aqua water could almost be the Caribbean, and the sunset over the Duirinish peninsula is as fine as any on Skye. From the car park, it's a one-mile walk to the beaches, with a few streams to hop over and some muddy fields to traverse, so bring appropriate footwear. It's possible to walk out to treeless Lampay Island at low tide; keep an eye on the water level for your return.

Duirinish peninsula

MAP PAGE 26

Much of the **Duirinish peninsula**, west of Dunvegan, is inaccessible to all except walkers prepared to scale or skirt the area's twin flat-topped basalt peaks: Healabhal Bheag

Claigan Coral Beaches

(1604ft) and Healabhal Mhor (1545ft). The mountains are better known as **MacLeod's Tables** – the story goes that the MacLeod chief held a royal feast on the lower of the two for James V.

Colbost Croft Museum

MAP PAGE 26
Colbost village.
www.dunveganmuseums.co.uk. Charge.
Local history plus information about nineteenth-century crofting is told through displays of news cuttings in this restored traditional blackhouse, four miles up the road from Dunvegan. A guide is usually on hand to answer questions, and the peat fire is often lit. At the time of writing, **Colbost** remains closed following storm damage. While there are plans to reopen, no concrete date has been set. Please check the website for updates.

Glendale

MAP PAGE 26
West from Loch Dunvegan, the broad, green sweep of **Glendale** feels instantly wilder after Dunvegan. Its moment in history came in 1882, when local crofters staged a rent strike against their landlords, the MacLeods. Five locals, who became known as the "Glendale Martyrs", were given two-month prison sentences, and in 1904 the crofters became the first owner-occupiers in the Highlands.

Neist Point Lighthouse

MAP PAGE 26
At the end of a narrow, single-track road (watch out for errant sheep) past Waterstein village, is a footpath out to Skye's most westerly spot, with its severe cliffs formed of basalt columns. The gleaming white and beige **Neist Point Lighthouse** sits precariously atop this spectacular end-of-the-world headland. The cliffs are home to seabirds like gannets and razorbills, and not only are there wonderful views to the Western Isles, but you might even spot dolphins and, if you're really lucky, the few remaining whales of the west coast pod of orcas. Allow around 45 minutes to complete the walk there and back from the car park.

The west coast of Duirinish

MAP PAGE 26
Another bumpy road leads down the west coast of Duirinish to Ramasaig, continuing five miles to the deserted village of Lorgill where, on August 4, 1830, every crofter was ordered to board the *Midlothian* in Loch Snizort and taken to Nova Scotia or to prison (those over the age of 70 were sent to the poorhouse). It's a great place for walkers, though, with easy, blustery footpaths that wind down to the coast and around the peninsula. Just off the main path, **Ollisdal Bothy** is one of the exceptional Mountain Bothies Association (MBA, www.mountainbothies.org.uk) properties and – after a re-roofing in late 2021 following storm damage – is a good place to spend a night in the wild without being exposed to the elements. The rudimentary accommodation is free, although donations to the organization are welcome. It lacks electricity or running water which, for most folk, is part of the allure. Bring firewood, plenty of water, sleeping bags and warm clothes.

Dun Beag Broch

MAP PAGE 26
Dun Beag Broch is one of the best-preserved prehistoric sites on Skye. Given the typical topography of Skye, you'd be forgiven for thinking that the broch was a basalt outcrop at first glance, cloaked in grass and surrounded by loose rocks. The brochs were large circular houses built of stone and suited to enduring harsh storms. This one is thought to be around 2000 years old, although it may have been inhabited up until the early eighteenth century.

Shops

Isle of Skye Brewing Company

MAP PAGE 26

Uig harbour. www.skyeale.com.

In 1992, a few Skye residents joked that the only solution to the island's poor standard of beers would be to brew their own. Three years later, those same locals set up this brewery, and these days any self-respecting Skye pub has their ales on tap. You can pop into their brewery in Uig to have a taster and pick up a bottle or two.

Isle of Skye Distillers

MAP PAGE 26

Rathad na Slignich, Portree. www.isleofskyedistillers.com.

Portree's very own distillery cranks out craft spirits such as its best-known flagship tipple: Misty Isle Gin. The concoction is one of a few that the team produce, infused with lemon, coriander and angelica plant, while the juniper berries are foraged from wild locations across the Isle of Skye. Gin school sessions are frequently held at the distillery for those who wish to learn more about making their own.

Skyeskyns

MAP PAGE 26

Stein. www.skyeskyns.co.uk.

The friendly folk at Scotland's only functioning tannery offer informative, witty tours explaining the whole process of leather-making. Upstairs, you can browse the final products, from surprisingly affordable woolly rugs right up to tailored gilets pushing the £1000 mark.

Skye Weavers

MAP PAGE 26

18 Fasach, Glendale. www.skyeweavers.co.uk.

Using a traditional bicycle-pedalled loom, the couple who run this small tweed and textile outfit make scarves, shawls, caps and home furnishings in various patterns and colours entirely from the wool of Skye's very own sheep. You can watch the weaving process in action and learn all about the production process from sheep to shawl.

Uig Pottery

MAP PAGE 26

Uig harbour. www.uigpottery.co.uk.

When you're based on an island with more than its fair share of natural beauty, it's little surprise to discover that most of the home-grown arts and crafts are inspired by those surrounds. Both sea and landscape influence the work that goes on in this working pottery, with the resulting ceramics on sale in the on-site shop. You can drop in to shop for tableware and other homeware, or simply to watch the creative process in action.

Cafés

Birch

MAP PAGE 26

Bayfield Road, Portree. www.birch-skye.co.

With lots of pale wood and handmade Cara Guthrie ceramics, this cool speciality coffee shop is the brainchild of Niall Munro, who wanted to bring a slice of Melbourne's café scene to Skye's capital. A monthly changing selection of coffee beans is hand-roasted in small batches and served alongside tempting baked goodies. A curated brunch menu includes the likes of miso noodle salad and poached eggs on sourdough with kimchi and chilli. ££

Café Arriba

MAP PAGE 26

Quay Brae, Portree. www.cafearriba.co.uk.

This local institution packs in the punters, who come for a gossip over coffee or tea served in large china pots as much as the globe-trotting lunch menu of home-made

Dulse & Brose

soups, wraps, pastas or creative fast food like wild-boar hot dogs. Good veggie options are available. ££

Jann's Cakes

MAP PAGE 26
Dunvegan. 01470 521 730.
This tiny place on Dunvegan's high street is a Skye legend for its cakes and home-made chocolates, and also prepares fresh sandwiches and soups (the smoked haddock chowder is good for the soul), plus hot organic meals like tagine and curries. Although it's not cheap, the quality of both taste and presentation is high. ££

Red Roof Skye

MAP PAGE 26
Holmisdale, 3 miles west of Colbost.
01470 511 304.
This cosy little café owned by an artist-musician couple has a loyal fan base for its superb lunches of local cheese or seafood platters with home-made breads, plus home baking with great coffee. Lunch specials are served until 3pm.

Occasionally holds intimate live music nights. £

Restaurants

Dulse & Brose

MAP PAGE 26
Bosville Hotel.
www.perlehotels.com.
The name translates to "seaweed and oatmeal" and the menu contains ingredients as varied and Scottish in provenance as it suggests. Drawing mainly on locally sourced meats and seafood, the menu is packed with dishes like ale-battered North Atlantic haddock and hand-cut chips or roast venison, all served in sophisticated surroundings. £££

Edinbane Inn

MAP PAGE 26
Edinbane, 8 miles east of Dunvegan.
www.edinbaneinn.co.uk.
Expect the likes of herb-crusted lamb with a root veg terrine and red wine jus served in the hotel's

Table with a view at *The Three Chimneys*

friendly bar that's also popular with locals. Live folk music sessions are held here, consisting of however many musicians turn up on Tues and Fri evenings and Sun afternoons from 3pm. £££

Loch Bay

MAP PAGE 26

Stein. www.lochbay-restaurant.co.uk.
Chef Michael Smith, formerly of *The Three Chimneys*, has taken up the mantle at this tiny, romantic dining room. Here, he whips up an elaborate, multiple-course Skye *fruits de mer* menu focusing on the bounty of the sea. There are two seating times available – 7pm or 7.30pm – and the culinary experience will set you back £140, but it's worth it for the exquisite Michelin-starred cuisine. Reservations essential. ££££

The Old School

MAP PAGE 26

Dunvegan. www.oldschoolrestaurant.co.uk.
The Old School has long been a favourite on the island. Traditional Scottish dishes, such as venison

haunch with whisky and honey sauce or hake with langoustine bisque, set the tone for the menus here. Raw stone walls and an open fire add character to a lofty and rather smart dining room. Live traditional music shakes things up every other Saturday. £££

Scorrybreac

MAP PAGE 26

Bosville Terrace. www.scorrybreac.com.
Scorrybreac consists of just eight tables in what could be somebody's front room, but is in fact one of Skye's most exciting restaurants. Chef Calum Munro serves a tasting menu (£95) featuring the likes of Staffin mackerel and coffee-seared venison in charmingly intimate quarters. It's no surprise that it got a nod from Michelin just months after opening. ££££

The Three Chimneys

MAP PAGE 26

Colbost. www.threechimneys.co.uk.
The Three Chimneys is the undisputed culinary heavyweight of Skye. At the vanguard of the island's foodie revolution, head chef Scott Davies draws on the natural larder of the Scottish Highlands and Islands to create exquisite à la carte dishes for discerning diners. Book the Kitchen Table experience (tasting menu £120) for a first-row seat to the culinary theatre unfolding before you. Reservations are, unsurprisingly, essential. ££££

Uig Hotel Restaurant

MAP PAGE 26

Uig. www.uig-hotel-skye.com.
Hearty local and seasonal fare is the main concern of the chefs at *Uig Hotel*'s pleasant restaurant. There's an authentic Scottish vibe throughout, right down to the tartan carpets. Classics like Scottish salmon, haddock fillet in Skye ale batter, or Highland red deer give a sense of what's in store. The whisky sour treacle tart's not a bad way to round things off either. ££££

Pubs and bars

The Ferry Inn

MAP PAGE 26

Uig. www.theferryinnskye.com.

This sophisticated, luxury inn has three en-suite doubles above one of Skye's best pubs. The long, impressive bar was made from elm wood salvaged from the Clan Donald estate, and the cask Isle of Skye Brewing Co ales are brewed just a few hundred yards away. Rustles up a decent meal and has an excellent pub garden with views towards the Waternish peninsula.

Isles Inn

MAP PAGE 26

Somerled Square. 01478 612 129.

With its log fire and flagstone floors, this inviting pub in the centre of Portree hosts the occasional ceilidh band, getting people up on their feet and dancing. Alongside Skye ales, you

can find some of the local spirits, like Talisker whisky and Misty Isle gin. No-nonsense pub grub is also available for around a tenner.

Merchant Bar

MAP PAGE 26

Bosville Hotel. www.dulsebrose.co.uk.

Classy and minimalist pub in wood and stone, *Merchant Bar* is the best boozer in Portree, serving Skye beers and a wealth of whiskies in an understated, cool space. The bar huddles up alongside the *Dulse & Brose* restaurant in the *Bosville Hotel*.

Stein Inn

MAP PAGE 26

Stein. www.thesteininn.co.uk.

This eighteenth-century waterfront inn – the oldest on Skye – is as traditional as you would hope. Come for local ales, an impressive array of malts, and uncomplicated dishes like beer-battered Mallaig haddock and chips.

Uig Hotel

Skye: Sleat, the Cuillin, Minginish and Raasay

While Skye ranks among Scotland's most-visited destinations, with all the summer coach tours and crowded hotspots that suggests, many of the island's most underrated – and lesser-visited – sights lie to the south of the island. This half of Scotland's second-largest island also has twelve Munros to bag, all clustered together in the Cuillin ridge and its surrounding peaks. These towering mountains dominate both the island and the attention of hikers and climbers throughout the year; you'll need experience and determination to conquer them all. Beyond its more obvious charms, the south of Skye also has underappreciated castles, natural wonders and excellent wildlife-spotting opportunities, too. And if the summer squeeze becomes unbearable, there's always the peaceful Isle of Raasay off the east coast, which is worth a detour at any time of year.

Kyleakin

MAP PAGE 38
Bus #55 from Broadford.
The **Skye Bridge** that rendered the ferry crossing redundant in 1995 has been a mixed blessing for **Kyleakin** (pronounced "ka*la*kin"). On the one hand, the old port village is now often bypassed entirely; on the other, this puts less of a strain on its neat centre, even in high season. Curiously, it's also evolved into a backpackers' hangout. Colourful boats bob in the harbour, above which looms the jagged ruins of **Caisteal Maol**, a fifteenth-century castle atop a hill.

Eilean Bàn

MAP PAGE 38
The bridge has not been as kind to **Eilean Bàn**, an island from which the bridge leapfrogs over Loch Alsh. From 1968 to 1969, its lighthouse keeper's cottage was briefly the home of Gavin Maxwell, author of *Ring of Bright Water*.

The island now serves as a **nature reserve** and can be visited on tours booked through the Eilean Bàn Trust (enquiries@eileanban.org).

Sleat peninsula

MAP PAGE 38
Bus #152 from Portree.
Thanks to the CalMac ferry from Mallaig to **Armadale**, many people's introduction to Skye is the **Sleat peninsula** (pronounced "Slate") at the southern tip of the island. The irony is that it's unlike almost anywhere else hereabouts: this uncharacteristically fertile pocket of the island is branded "The Garden of Skye".

Armadale Castle, Gardens and Museum

MAP PAGE 38
On A851, half a mile north of Armadale.
Bus #152 from Portree.
www.armadalecastle.com. Charge.
Branded as **Clan Donald Skye** on account of its former inhabitants,

Sea kayaking near Armadale

Armadale Castle, situated around a mile north of the ferry terminal, is the shell of the neo-Gothic seat of the MacDonald clan; the laird moved into the gardeners' cottage when the kelp fertilizer market collapsed in the 1920s. Intended as an account of the clan, its modern **Museum of the Isles** is actually more interesting for its perspectives on Highland history, with excellent sections on the Jacobite period and its aftermath, featuring Bonnie Prince Charlie keepsakes such as his shoe buckles worn in battle at Culloden, and a couple of cannonballs fired at the castle by HMS *Dartmouth*, sent by William III. Just as appealing is the castle's forty-acre wooded **garden**, where you might get the opportunity to try your hand at traditional country pursuits archery and clay-pigeon shooting.

South Skye Sea Kayak

MAP PAGE 38
Kilmore, 2 miles north of Armadale Castle. Bus #152 from Portree. www.southskyeseakayak.co.uk. Charge.
One of the most liberating ways to explore Skye's remarkable coastline is by sea kayak. All tours by **South Skye Sea Kayak** are led by experienced, qualified instructors and there's the freedom to choose which part of the nearby coast you paddle to, with secluded coves, deserted white-sand beaches and mirror-still sea lochs all accessible during the half-day and full-day guided excursions.

Torabhaig Distillery

MAP PAGE 38
Teangue. Bus #152 from Portree. www.torabhaig.com. Charge.
For a long time, there had only ever been one working, legal, single malt Scotch whisky distillery on the Isle of Skye. Then along came **Torabhaig**. Built into a renovated old farmstead, the distillery started producing spirits in 2017, and come 2020, some of the earliest batches of Torabhaig single malt were finally allowed to call themselves whisky (three years being the minimum permitted maturation period). Guided tours of the facility highlight just how you can turn an old farmstead into a traditional distillery and make a good dram from it.

Isleornsay

MAP PAGE 38
Bus #152 from Portree.

Having retired as Skye's main fishing port, **Isleornsay** (Eilean Iarmain), six miles north of Armadale, is these days just a pretty, secluded village. Come for the views: out across the bay to a necklace of seaweed-encrusted rocks and the tidal **Isle of Ornsay**, all against a dramatic backdrop of Highland peaks marching across the mainland.

The west coast of Sleat

MAP PAGE 38

A narrow, up-and-down single-track road loops off the A851 to the wilder west coast of Sleat. Turning at Kilbeg, you ascend over moorland past somnambulant sheep before arriving into **Tarskavaig**, scattered behind a little beach. Further up the coast, the stony beach

at **Tokavaig** is overlooked by ruined **Dunscaith Castle** and enjoys views over the Cuillin range – this cragged corner of Sleat offers a superb panorama of the mountains (if the weather plays ball).

Broadford

MAP PAGE 38
Buses #152 and #155 from Portree.

Skye's second-largest village, **Broadford** (An t-Àth Leathann), strung out along the main road, has a traffic problem and a charm bypass. It is indeed handy for its full quota of facilities – not least a large supermarket and 24-hour fuel – but you won't want to hang around here for too long. Fill the tank, load up the boot with supplies and go explore the island. If you do stick around though, keep an eye out for otters in the sea, which have been known to cavort around this area.

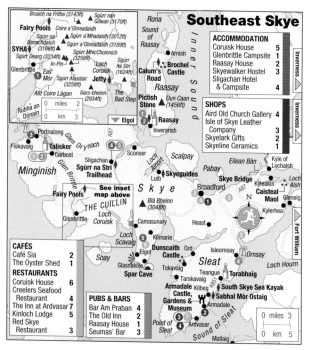

Skye Creative Trail

Skye has a growing crop of independent artisans, each offering a great opportunity to pick up some unique, high-quality local arts and crafts. Some studios and workshops offer a free tour without prior arrangement; the perfect remedy to a rainy day. The Skye Creative Trail was the natural result of a need to correlate the islanders' different creative endeavours in one place. Art Skye (www.art-skye.co.uk) produces an excellent map so that you can visit nearby creatives and shop their work, wherever you may be on the island. However, most places have limited opening hours during the winter months.

The Cuillin and Red Hills

MAP PAGE 38

The **Cuillin Range** has razor-edge ridges, slopes that plummet down to scree fields, and lonely lochs imbued with a magical quality. Small wonder that, for many, these spectacular mountains are Skye's biggest draw. When – if – the cloud disperses, these mighty peaks dominate the island. There are three **approaches**: from the south, on foot or by boat from Elgol; on foot from *Sligachan Hotel* to the north; or on foot from Glenbrittle to the west. Glen Sligachan is one of the most popular routes as it marks a natural boundary between the round-topped **Red Cuillin** (sometimes referred to as the Red Hills) to the east and the Cuillin themselves – sometimes known as the **Black Cuillin** on account of their coarse-grained jagged gabbro. With twelve Munros between them, these mountains are not to be messed with. There are around five fatalities a year and many Black Cuillin trails are for experienced mountaineers only, no matter how easy Danny Macaskill makes it look on YouTube. In winter, that means knowing your way around a pair of crampons and an ice-axe.

Elgol

MAP PAGE 38
Bus #55 from Kyle of Lochalsh.
The road to **Elgol** (Ealaghol), a miniscule village draped across the tip of the Strathaird peninsula, is one of the most impressive on Skye, swooping into the heart of the Red Cuillin to culminate in beautiful views of the Small Isles above Elgol pier. Follow the footpath south into the fields along the headland for some of the best Cuillin views anywhere on the island. Continue along the path to **Spar Cave**, which is reached via a steep descent and only accessible at low tide. This gloomy cavern is surprisingly high-ceilinged and filled with fascinating calcified shapes that

Beach of Elgol looking towards the Cuillins

Sligachan Old Bridge

have formed over millennia of steady water percolation through the limestone. Be sure to check the tide times before attempting to head underground and make sure to leave plenty of room to get back out.

Loch Coruisk

MAP PAGE 38

The chief reason for visiting Elgol is to hop on board a boat, whether as part of a wildlife cruise or a trip across Loch Scavaig, to visit **Loch Coruisk**. This isolated, glacial loch is cradled among some of the highest peaks of the Cuillin and is a superb trip, about an hour by boat then up to a half-day ashore. A path traces the shores of the loch, but good footwear is a must. The boat ride itself is worthwhile to see the foreboding peaks looming ever closer, and you may also catch a glimpse of colonies of seals lolloping about on the rocks.

Sligachan

MAP PAGE 38

Buses #52 and #154 from Portree.

Many walkers hop on a boat simply to begin hikes in the Red Hills or carry them over the pass into **Glen Sligachan**. However, the time-honoured approach to this remote glen is on foot from *Sligachan Hotel*, a popular hikers' base with a good bar and restaurant and a garden scattered with picnic tables. Be sure to check out the photogenic **Sligachan Old Bridge**, overlooking the frothing, boulder-strewn river.

Glenbrittle

MAP PAGE 38

Yet another route into the peaks is from **Glenbrittle** on the west side. The valley skirts the most spectacular peaks of the Cuillin, a semicircle of mountains wrapping around Loch Coruisk, before it runs to a beach at **Loch Brittle**. One of the least demanding walks is a five-mile round trip (3hr) from *Glenbrittle Campsite* up Coire Làgan to a lochan squeezed between stern rock faces. An equally good reason to visit is the **Fairy Pools**, one of Britain's most celebrated wild swimming destinations. The scenery is superb as the river tumbles beneath peaks. The downside is the water temperature: 8–10°C at best, plus it gets incredibly busy during the summer. The pools are signposted from Glumagan Na Sithichean car park.

Rubha an Dùnain

MAP PAGE 38

Often overlooked, due to the imposing nature of the Cuillin and allure of the Fairy Pools, is the empty peninsula of **Rubha an Dùnain**. While nobody lives here now, the remains of a once-thriving settlement still mark the landscape at the peninsula tip, including **Iron Age** and **Neolithic foundations**, and even a **Viking Canal**, built to bring longboats out of the water at high tide. Human activity ceased here with the Clearances in the 1860s. It can be reached on a 2.5-mile (1.5hr) walk from *Glenbrittle Campsite*.

Minginish

MAP PAGE 38

Bus #154 from Portree.

If the Cuillin has slipped into the mist for the day and you have your own transport, while away a happy afternoon exploring the **Minginish** nearby. This rugged peninsula is accessible via roads from both Sligachan and Glenbrittle.

Talisker Whisky Distillery

MAP PAGE 38

By Loch Harport, Carbost, Bus #154 from Portree. 01478 614 308, email: talisker@diageo.com. Charge for tours.

One ideal wet-weather activity is a guided tour of the **Talisker Whisky Distillery**, which produces a range of full-bodied single malts often containing a peppery, peat smoke profile over subtler flavours like vanilla. Skye's first – and up until 2017, only – distillery hugs the shores of Loch Harport at **Carbost**; not, confusingly, at the village of Talisker itself, which lies on the west coast of Minginish. Whisky

Talisker Whisky Distillery, the newest kid in town

fanatics might consider splashing out for the excellent two-hour Talisker Masterclass tour, which includes tastings of five different single malts produced on site.

Isle of Raasay

MAP PAGE 38

The hilly, fourteen-mile-long island of **Raasay** (Ratharsair) offers an insight into what Skye may have been like before tourism took off. A 25-minute ferry ride from Sconser, this rocky sliver offers plenty of walks and rich flora and fauna, including golden eagles, snipe, orchids and the unique Raasay vole, not to mention the castaway thrill of a small island. Most visitors arrive as foot passengers. If you bring a car, be aware there's no petrol station. The ferry docks in Churchton Bay, near **Inverarish**, the island's (tiny) main village sheltered among thick woods on the southwest coast. There isn't

much in the village beyond a local shop-cum-post office, though the Isle of Raasay Distillery can be found along the road to the dock.

Isle of Raasay Distillery

MAP PAGE 38
Borodale House.
www.raasaydistillery.com. Charge.
Despite the growing number of whisky distilleries around this part of Scotland, Raasay never had a legal one until 2017, when the **Isle of Raasay Distillery** turned on the taps. Specializing in Hebridean single malt Scotch, using water from a Celtic well beneath the distillery, the first official whisky came of age in 2020. Gin is distilled here too, and you can learn all about the production process, as well as a tasting session on one of the regular guided tours. There's also a special whisky and chocolate tasting tour; the chocolates are infused with whisky.

Narrow, winding roads on Raasay

Raasay in history

Raasay's woes began after the staunchly Jacobite MacLeods of Lewis sent a hundred local men and 26 pipers to Culloden. Bonnie Prince Charlie later spent a miserable night on Raasay in a "mean low hut" during his flight and swore to replace the turf cottages with proper stone houses (he never did). Raasay was practically destroyed in 1746 by vengeful government troops in the aftermath of the 1745 uprising and the Young Pretender's escape. Then, when the MacLeods were forced to sell up in 1843, the Clearances started in earnest. In 1921, seven ex-servicemen and their families from neighbouring Rona illegally squatted crofts on Raasay, and were imprisoned, sparking a public outcry. As a result, both islands were bought by the government the following year. Rona now has three permanent residents while Raasay's population hovers around 160.

Raasay House

MAP PAGE 38
A short walk from the ferry pier.
www.raasay-house.co.uk.
Raasay House is the focal point of the island, around which much of Raasay's history took place and where much of the activity currently happens. The present building was started in 1747 to replace the original MacLeod clan house, which had been destroyed. Now, it serves as hotel, bar, restaurant and outdoor tour operator, all rolled into one. Among the activities on offer (Easter–Oct, weather-dependent other months) are sea kayaking, rock climbing, guided walks and canyoning. Boat trips around Raasay or north to Rona island (2hr) and sailing are also available. Bike rental is available here too. Nearby, a small Pictish stone is scored with original carvings – still readily visible after all these years.

Dun Caan

MAP PAGE 38
Most visitors come to walk into the island's interior, a rugged terrain of sandstone in the south giving way to gneiss landscapes further north. The obvious destination is the flat-top volcanic plug of **Dun Caan** (1456ft) where Boswell "danced a Highland dance" when he visited with Dr Johnson in 1773. The five-mile trail to the top is easy to follow; a splendid trek along the burn through forest behind Inverarish, culminating in epic 360-degree views of Skye and the mainland from the summit. The quickest return is down the northwest slope, but you can also reach the ferry terminal via the path tracing the southeast shore, passing the **abandoned crofters' village** of Hallaig. Keep your eyes peeled for roaming eagles overhead and the odd scuttling grouse.

North Raasay

MAP PAGE 38
On a fine day, the north provides fine views across to the Cuillin, Portree and the Trotternish peninsula. Where the road dips to the east coast, the stark remains of fifteenth-century **Brochel Castle** come into view, peering solemnly over the shore. The final two-mile stretch of the road to Arnish is known as **Calum's Road**: in the 1960s the council refused to extend the road, so Calum MacLeod decided to build it himself. It took him ten years, and by the time he'd finished, he and his wife were the only people left in the village.

Walking in the Cuillin

Ordnance Survey Explorer map 411

For many walkers and climbers, there's nowhere in Britain to beat the mighty Cuillin. The main ridge is just eight miles long, but with its immediate neighbours it is made up of over thirty peaks, twelve of them Munros. Those intent on tackling the complete **Cuillin ridge traverse** usually start at **Gars-bheinn**, at the southeastern tip, and finish at **Sgùrr nan Gillean** (3167ft), descending to the famous *Sligachan Hotel* for a well-earned pint. The entire journey takes a minimum of sixteen hours, which either means a very long day or two days and a bivouac. The time spent on the mountain requires as much mental agility as physical. A period of settled weather is pretty much essential, and only experienced walkers and climbers should attempt it. Take note of all the usual safety precautions and be aware that **compasses** are unreliable in the Cuillin, due to the magnetic nature of the rocks. At least nine of the peaks involve a Grade 2 scramble or higher. If you're unsure of what that entails, it might be a good idea to hire a guide who can provide ropes and safety gear, as well as expertise.

If you're based in Glenbrittle, one of the more straightforward walks is the five-mile round trip from the campsite up **Coire Làgan**, to a crystal-cold lochan squeezed in among the sternest of rockfaces. If you simply want to bag one or two of the peaks, several corries provide relatively painless approaches to the central Munros. From the *SYHA hostel*, a path heads west along the southern bank of the stream that tumbles down from the **Coire a' Ghreadaidh**. From the corrie, you can climb up to An Dorus, the obvious gap in the ridge, then ascend **Sgùrr a' Mhadaidh** (3012ft) or **Sgùrr a' Ghreadaidh** (3189ft) to the south. Alternatively, before Coire a' Ghreadaidh, you can veer south to the **Coir' an Eich**, from which you can easily climb **Sgùrr a'**

Banachdaich (3166ft) via its western ridge. To the south of the youth hostel, the road crosses another stream, with another path along its southern banks. This path swerves west past the impressive **Eas Mòr** (Great Waterfall), before heading up to the **Coire na Banachdaich**. The pass above the corrie is the main one over to Loch Coruisk, but also gives access to **Sgùrr Dearg**, best known for its great view of the **Inaccessible Pinnacle** or "In-Pin" (3234ft). It doesn't actually live up to the name, but Scotland's most difficult Munro requires good rock-climbing skills. Back at Eas Mòr, paths head off for Coire Làgan, by far the most popular corrie thanks to its steep sides and tiny lochan.

If you'd like a good hike through the mountains but aren't too bothered about bagging the peaks, there are a couple of much more manageable routes to take you into the heart of the Cuillin range that involve little-to-no scrambling. From *Sligachan Hotel*, you can pick up the Sgurr na Stri trailhead that passes along **Glen Sligachan**. When the path forks, the left route heads down towards Camasunary, where there is a bothy by the beach, while the right-hand path winds over a ridge and down the other side to **Loch Coruisk**. From here, a path skirts the headland to Camasunary, which requires the negotiation of a tough section called **The Bad Step**, an overhanging rock with a 30ft drop to the sea, or you can catch the boat to Elgol in summer (reserve a seat in advance; see page 39).

Blà Bheinn is not part of the main Black Cuillin range, but it is an outlier Munro peak. The hike to the top is one of the less technical ascents, with only a small amount of scrambling required near the summit. From the peak, there are fantastic 360-degree views on cloud-free days. There's also a handy car park at the trailhead along the B8083. If you're unsure about any hike or want help, hire a guide: try Skye Guides (www.skyeguides.co.uk). For anybody considering attempting the entire Cuillin ridge traverse, be prepared for a vetting from guides to ensure you have the experience required to complete the route.

Shops

Aird Old Church Gallery

MAP PAGE 38
Aird of Sleat.
www.airdoldchurchgallery.org.
Right at the tip of the Sleat
Peninsula, an old church has been
reimagined as an art gallery and
shop displaying watercolours and
prints by artist Peter McDermott
and handmade jewellery by his
wife Jane. Both creatives produce
work that manages to capture the
raw, wild essence of Skye's skies
and shoreline – both of which
provide an inspiring backdrop to
the church.

Isle of Skye Leather Company

MAP PAGE 38
The Old Ticket Office, Armadale Pier.
www.isleofskyeleather.com.
A dinky shop at the end of
Armadale Pier, the *Isle of Skye
Leather* is packed with high-
quality leather belts, wallets, bags,
sporrans, moccasins, bracelets,

The Oyster Shed

guitar straps and reindeer-hide
rugs, all handcrafted by owner
Robbie. Many are Celtic designs,
celebrating the heritage of the
Highlands and Islands.

Skyelark Gifts

MAP PAGE 38
Armadale Pier. www.skyelark.co.uk.
Bringing together a broad selection
of handcrafted items made on the
island, *Skyelark Gifts* is a good stop
on the way to, or from, Armadale
Pier. It is also the spot where
fantastic photography by former
island resident GrumpyGeorge can
be bought.

Skyeline Ceramics

MAP PAGE 38
Beside the A87 on the southern approach
to Broadford. www.skyelineceramics.com.
Of the many artisanal workshops
and independent craft studios in
Broadford, *Skyeline Ceramics* is well
worth a stop. Lesley works with
two types of clay: buff stoneware
for bowls and other vessels, and
translucent porcelain for more
intricate pieces. Each piece is

Skyelark Gifts

handmade, making it unique from any other that she produces.

Cafés

Café Sia

MAP PAGE 38

On the A87, Broadford. www.cafesia.co.uk.
The best pizzas on Skye, wood-fired to perfection, and probably among the best coffee too. *Café Sia* also serves breakfast, and the outdoor deck has decent views out towards the Red Cuillin. The café is located just off the A87. £

The Oyster Shed

MAP PAGE 38

Carbost. www.theoysterman.co.uk.
Less a café, more of an artisanal food shack, *The Oyster Shed* serves up some of the finest – and best-value – seafood you're likely to find anywhere on Skye. Order the Hebridean lobster, crab claws in garlic butter, grilled scallops or classic fish and chips, either to take away or eat perched on one

of the wooden barrels overlooking Loch Harport. ££

Restaurants

Coruisk House

MAP PAGE 38

Elgol. www.coruiskhouse.com.
Set in a traditional croft house, this intimate Michelin-listed restaurant offers a taste of Skye through its daily-changing four-course set menu (£75) – think hand-dived scallops from Sconser, mussels from Loch Eishort, Edinbane wild venison. Reservations are essential. Four chic rooms are also available, including two suites with free-standing rolltop baths. ££££

Creelers Seafood Restaurant

MAP PAGE 38

Lower Harrapool.
www.skye-seafood-restaurant.co.uk.
No fuss, no highfalutin' foams, this wee restaurant is all about local seafood simply but

Hake fillet at *Kinloch Lodge*

superbly prepared, such as a rich bouillabaisse, sautéed crayfish tails or mussels in dry white wine, butter, garlic and parsley. £££

The Inn at Ardvasar

MAP PAGE 38

Ardvasar, 0.5 miles south of Armadale. www.the-inn-at-aird-a-bhasair.co.uk.
This pretty little inn – one of the oldest on Skye – serves up pub classics with a contemporary twist, all made using local, in-seasonal produce. Dishes may include Aberdeen Angus sirloin steak, Eilean Iarmain estate venison or baked fillet of hake. £££

Kinloch Lodge

MAP PAGE 38

Sleat. www.kinloch-lodge.co.uk.
The island's smartest hotel remains the home of Lord and Lady MacDonald of MacDonald, and as such is furnished with antiques and clan mementos. As famous is the food, which is considered the pinnacle of Skye's gourmet scene.

Try the daily-changing three-course set menu or succinct lunch menus, which showcase super-fresh island ingredients. Advance booking is essential. ££££

Red Skye Restaurant

MAP PAGE 38

Breakish. www.redskyerestaurant.co.uk.
The unusual high-ceilinged dining space at *Red Skye Restaurant* occupies a schoolhouse. The seasonal menu concentrates on traditional Scottish dishes, such as whisky-infused mussels in a white wine and garlic sauce, or Black Isle beef and red wine jus. Payment by cash or cheque only. £££

Pubs and bars

Bar Am Praban

MAP PAGE 38

Near Isleornsay.
www.eileaniarmain.co.uk/bar-am-praban.
This homey, wood-panelled drinking den enjoys an enviable

location smack bang on the Sleat peninsula coast. There's a good selection of whiskies and locally brewed Skye beers on offer. Make the most of fine weather with a leisurely pint in the peaceful beer garden overlooking the water. *Bar Am Praban* also serves a small menu packed with excellent, rich food, including the likes of perfectly grilled steaks, fresh lobster, fish and chips, and a decent cheese board. ££

The Old Inn

MAP PAGE 38

Carbost. www.theoldinnskye.co.uk.
Hugging the scenic shores of Loch Harport, the historic *Old Inn* is a popular watering hole frequented by locals, hikers and day-trippers on the Minginish peninsula. The kitchen rustles together consistently decent bar meals, with plenty of pan-Scottish staples like haggis, neaps and tatties in a whisky cream sauce. The pub also hosts regular live traditional music sessions, so check the events schedule ahead of your visit to experience an extra dose of Hebridean culture. ££

Raasay House

MAP PAGE 38

A short walk from ferry pier.
www.raasay-house.co.uk.
The MacLeods' rebuilt manor is the only place to eat or drink on Raasay, in the convivial bar-restaurant. But the lack of competition doesn't seem to impact the quality of food or service here. The cosy space is a great place to sit with a pint after a day in the great outdoors, and there's an outdoor terrace for warm days. ££

Seumas' Bar

MAP PAGE 38

On the A87. www.sligachan.co.uk.
This long-standing launchpad for hikers sits in the shadow of the magnificent Cuillin peaks. Connected to the *Sligachan Hotel*, the barn-like *Seumas' Bar* serves real ale on tap from the on-site Cuillin Brewery and is stocked with a whopping 400-plus whiskies. Thankfully, it also plates up hearty dishes like venison stew and rib of beef with haggis to soak up the booze. Bring some insect repellent in summer, as the midges are as famous as the view. ££

SKYE: SLEAT, THE CUILLIN, MINGINISH AND RAASAY

The Old Inn beer garden

The Small Isles

Seen from southern Skye or the west coast of the Highlands, the Small Isles – Rùm, Eigg, tiny Muck and narrow Canna – lie scattered in a silver-grey sea like a siren call to adventure. Each island has a population numbering the hundreds and its own unique identity and atmosphere. After centuries of being passed between owners, most islands have stabilized into tight-knit communities of crofters. While Muck is still privately owned, Eigg was bought out by its islanders in 1997, ending more than 150 years of property speculation, while other islands have been bequeathed to national agencies: Rùm, by far the largest and most visited of the group, passed to the Nature Conservancy Council (now NatureScot) in 1957; and Canna has been in the hands of the National Trust for Scotland since 1981. Many people visit the archipelago on a day-trip, but the Small Isles deserve longer. They are an opportunity to experience some off-grid island life while walking, birdwatching or simply taking in the pristine seascapes. Public transport on the islands is non-existent, but regular ferries mean you're not as cut off as the atmosphere suggests.

White-tailed eagle

Rùm

MAP PAGE 52

After almost a century as the "Forbidden Isle" – the exclusive sporting estate of self-made Lancastrian industrialists, the Bulloughs – **Rùm** opened up. Indeed, since it passed to NatureScot (formerly Scottish Natural Heritage) in 1957, visitors are positively encouraged. Many come to hike the eight-mile **Rùm Cuillin Ridge Walk**, tracking a crown of peaks that are modest by Skye's standards – the summit of Askival is only 2663ft – but every bit as impressive in looks. And in recent years, crofting land has been released as NatureScot tries to encourage a community.

Kinloch

MAP PAGE 52

Most of the island's twenty-plus inhabitants live around **Kinloch**

Kinloch Castle

on the east coast, and many are employed by NatureScot, which runs the island as a National Nature Reserve. NatureScot has reintroduced native woodland and **white-tailed eagles**, most of which promptly flew to neighbouring islands. **Rùm** is renowned for its **Manx shearwaters**, which nest in burrows on high peaks. You can learn about the flora and fauna in an unmanned **visitor centre** halfway between the wharf and castle.

Kilmory Bay

MAP PAGE 52

Rùm's best beach is located in the north of the island at **Kilmory Bay**, where a ruined settlement serves as a reminder of when the inhabitants of Rùm were cruelly kicked off the island during the Clearances in 1826. Reaching this sandy crescent involves a flattish walk on tracks through Kinloch and then Kilmory glens (10 miles, 5hr return from Kinloch). Bear in mind that Rùm is the wettest of the Small Isles, and is notorious for midges, so come prepared. You're likely to encounter wild goats, ponies and Highland cattle on Rùm, as well as red deer, which are so numerous that there's a research base here investigating the specie.

Kinloch Castle

MAP PAGE 52
Kinloch, signposted 15min walk from the ferry. Currently closed to the public.

Rùm's main calling card has long been **Kinloch Castle**, but the future of this former hunting lodge is on shaky ground. Built at huge expense in 1900 – the red sandstone was shipped in from Dumfriesshire and the soil for the gardens from Ayrshire – its decor is sheer Edwardian decadence. It's also appealingly bonkers. From the galleried hall, with its tiger rugs, stags' heads and giant Japanese incense burners, to the Soho snooker table in the Billiard Room, the interior is packed with technical gizmos accumulated by Sir George Bullough (1870–1939), the spendthrift son of self-made millionaire Sir John Bullough, who bought the island as a sporting estate in 1888. It was only used for a few weeks each autumn, when guests were woken at eight each morning by a bagpiper; later, an orchestrion (an electrically driven barrel organ) that was made for Queen Victoria would grind out pre-dinner ditties like *The Ride of the Valkyries* and *Ma Blushin' Rosie*. In more recent years, the property gained a new lease of life as a hostel, before falling empty in 2015. The damp walls, furniture rips and ceiling cracks may add to the ramshackle charm, but restoration works are estimated at over £10 million. The castle's owners, NatureScot, had been in talks to sell the former pleasure palace to multimillionaire Brexiteer and political donor Jeremy Hosking, who had hoped to turn it into a hotel. However, amid concerns from locals over access to the surrounding land and the impact of proposed plans on the community, Hosking pulled out of the deal in 2023. For now, the question of what's next for the castle remains unanswered.

Walks from Kinloch

MAP PAGE 52

Two gentle waymarked walks wend from Kinloch into the surrounding countryside. The **Northside Nature Trail** (1hr) loops via Kinloch Glen and is signposted from the visitor centre. In addition, a forest trail

from the ferry dock reaches an otter hide (15min return walk) then continues to the abandoned hamlet of Port na Caranean (40min on from the hide). The goal for hardened hikers, though, is the Rùm Cuillin Ridge Walk (see page 53).

Bullough Mausoleum

MAP PAGE 52

Harris, 8 miles southwest of Kinloch.

When the island's headcount peaked at 450 in 1791, the hamlet of **Harris** on the southwest coast (a 3–4hr walk from Kinloch) housed a crofting community. All that remains are ruined blackhouses, which makes the Neoclassical **Bullough Mausoleum** all the more extraordinary and incongruous. It was built by Sir George for his father and is, in fact, the second family mausoleum here; the first was lined with Italian marble, but dynamited after a friend remarked it looked like a public lavatory.

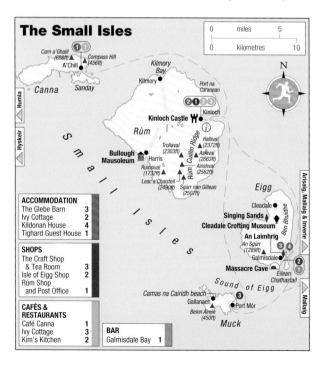

The Small Isles

0 — miles — 5
0 — kilometres — 10

Carn a'Ghaill (698ft)
A'Chill
Compass Hill (456ft)
Canna
Sanday
Kilmory Bay
Kilmory
Port na Caranean
Kinloch Castle
Kinloch
Rùm
Trollaval (2303ft)
Hallival (2372ft)
Askival (2663ft)
Bullough Mausoleum
Harris
Ruinsival (1732ft)
Ainshval (2562ft)
Leac a'Chaisteil (2490ft)
Sgùrr nan Gillean (2507ft)
Humla
Hyskeir
S m a l l   I s l e s
Eigg
Cleadale
Singing Sands
Cleadale Crofting Museum
An Laimhrig
An Sgùrr (1289ft)
Galmisdale
Massacre Cave
Eilean Chathastail
Sound of Eigg
Camas na Cairidh beach
Gallanach
Beinn Airein (450ft)
Port Mór
Muck
Arisaig, Mallaig & Inverie
Mallaig

ACCOMMODATION	
The Glebe Barn	3
Ivy Cottage	2
Kildonan House	4
Tighard Guest House	1

SHOPS	
The Craft Shop & Tea Room	3
Isle of Eigg Shop	2
Rùm Shop and Post Office	1

CAFÉS & RESTAURANTS	
Café Canna	1
Ivy Cottage	3
Kim's Kitchen	2

BAR	
Galmisdale Bay	1

Hiking in the Rùm Cuillin

Ordnance Survey Explorer map 397

Rùm's Cuillin may not be as famous as Skye's, but in fine weather, the lesser-known peaks offer equally exhilarating hiking possibilities. Whatever route you choose, be sure to take all the usual safety precautions, if for no other reason than the remoteness of the island means mobile phone coverage can be poor to non-existent.

The most popular walk is to traverse most or part of the **Cuillin Ridge**, around a twelve-hour round trip from Kinloch. The most frequent route is via Coire Dubh, then on to the saddle of Bealach Bairc-mheall. From here, you can either climb Barkeval to the west, or plump for **Hallival** (2372ft) southeast, which looks daunting but is only a mild scramble. South of Hallival, the ridge is grassy, but the north ridge of **Askival** (2663ft) needs to be taken carefully, sticking to the east side. Askival is the highest mountain on Rùm, and one of the island's two Corbetts (Scottish mountains between 2500ft and 3000ft). If you're thinking of heading back, or if the weather is closing in, Glen Dibidil provides an easy descent from here.

To continue along the ridge, head west to the double peak of **Trollaval** (or Trallval). The descent to Bealach an Fhuarain is steep, after which it's another scramble to reach the top of **Ainshval** (2562ft). Depending on the time and weather, you can continue along the ridge to **Sgùrr nan Gillean**, descend via Glen Dibidil and take the coastal path back to Kinloch, or skip the Sgùrr and go straight on to the last peak of the ridge, **Ruinsival**.

Eigg

MAP PAGE 52

Eigg – which measures just five miles by three – does little to conceal its volcanic origins. It is made of a basalt plateau, and a great stump of pitchstone lava, known as An Sgùrr, rises in the south. Eigg has an appealingly strong sense of community: its hundred-odd residents (alongside the Scottish Wildlife Trust) pulled off the first buyout of a Highlands estate in 1997, thereby ending Eigg's unhappy history of private ownership. The anniversary is celebrated with an all-night **ceilidh** on the weekend nearest June 12. Its other world-first is that its electricity grid is powered entirely by renewable sources.

Galmisdale

MAP PAGE 52

Ferries arrive into Galmisdale Bay, in the southeast of the island.

The much-awaited redesign of An Laimhrig is set to complete in 2023, with its clean architectural lines and huge swathes of glass framing ocean views. The community hub will

Galmisdale Bay on the Isle of Eigg

Laig beach on Eigg looking towards Rùm

bring together a café, bar, craft shop and the Eigg Adventures kayak- and bike-hire company. The project also includes new toilets and green electricity showers for campers. Head up through the woods for fine sea views, or track the shore south to see crofting ruins before the Sgùrr cliffs; the remains of Upper and Lower Grulin settlements. If the tide is low, you can scramble along the shore into Cathedral Cave or **Massacre Cave** (Uamh Fhraing), where all but one of Eigg's 396 inhabitants died in 1577, suffocated by the MacLeods of Skye, who lit a fire in the cave mouth. Bring a torch and prepare to feel spooked.

An Sgùrr

MAP PAGE 52

The UK's largest slab of pitchstone, **An Sgùrr** (1289ft) is ripe for a hike. The route up is not as daunting as the cliffs suggest; the path is signposted left from the main road, crossing boggy moor to approach the peak from the north via a saddle (3–4hr return). The reward: wonderful views to Muck and Rùm.

Cleadale

MAP PAGE 52

For an easy stroll, strike out for **Cleadale**, the main crofting settlement in north Eigg. It's spectacularly sited beneath the island's basalt ridge, **Ben Bhuidhe**, and above a beach known as Camas Sgiotaig, or the **Singing Sands**, because the quartz grains squeak underfoot. The views from here to the cloud-shrouded peaks of Rùm are unforgettable.

Cleadale Crofting Museum

MAP PAGE 52

Croft 6. Always open. Free, but donations are appreciated.

Poke your head into the community-run **Cleadale Crofting Museum** to see what life would have been like for the Campbell family, who moved here in 1907. Printouts provide context to the building's items, which include an old hot-water bottle, an original Singer sewing machine and hundreds of tools and cast-iron utensils laid out in the attic.

Muck

MAP PAGE 52

Barely two miles long, tiny **Muck** is the smallest and most southerly of the Small Isles. Low-lying and almost treeless, it is extremely fertile, so has more in common with Coll and Tiree than with its neighbours. Its name derives from *muc*, the Gaelic for "pig" (or possibly *muc mara*, "sea pig" or porpoise, which are plentiful in the sea around the island), and has long caused embarrassment to lairds – they preferred to call it the "Isle of Monk" because it briefly belonged to the medieval church.

Port Mór

MAP PAGE 52

Port Mór is the hub of all activity on Muck, where visitors arrive and just about all of the thirty or so residents live; that's less than one-tenth of the 320 who lived here in the early 1800s. A mile-long road connects Port Mór with the island's main farm, **Gallanach**, which overlooks rocky skerries on the north side. The nicest sandy **beach** is Camas na Cairidh, to the east of Gallanach. For a stiffer challenge, **Beinn Airein** (2hr return), in the southwest corner of the island, is worth climbing, despite being only 450ft above sea level. There's the reward of a 360-degree panorama of the surrounding islands and mainland from the summit.

Canna

MAP PAGE 52

At just five miles by one mile, the slender island of **Canna** has been managed as a **bird sanctuary** by the National Trust for Scotland (NTS) since 1938. There are no roads, just open moorland draped across a basalt ridge, and very few people now that the population has dwindled to fifteen. Neighbouring Sanday is only connected to Canna at low tide (see page 55), casting the tiny speck adrift when the sea rolls in. While Canna doesn't receive many visitors by ferry, plenty come by yacht for the best harbour in the Small Isles, a sheltered bay off Canna's main hamlet, A'Chill. Notwithstanding hikers, the largest proportion of visitors to Canna are twitchers, lured by the 157 species recorded here, including golden and white-tailed eagles, Manx shearwaters, razorbills and puffins on the cliffs at the western end. Up to 20,000 breeding seabirds nest here each year. There are also high cliffs along the entire northern and eastern edge of the island.

Compass Hill

MAP PAGE 52

Although less showy than the other Small Isles, the flat(ish) terrain is enjoyable for walking. You can circuit the entire island on a day-long hike (10hr; 12 miles), or from the dock it's about a mile across a grassy plateau to the cliffs on the north shore, and to **Compass Hill**, so-named because its high iron content distorts compasses. A mile west is **Carn a'Ghaill**, Canna's summit at a heady 688ft.

Repopulating Canna

In 2006, the NTS attempted to combat the dwindling population on Canna by advertising for people to come and rent two of the then-vacant properties on the island. The stipulation was for skilled manual workers, such as gardeners or builders, who could bring a new lease of vitality and upkeep to the island. Thousands responded, from as far afield as the US and India, and it looked like the gamble had paid off. However, the success was short-term and roughly a dozen residents left the island in 2011. Unable to increase the population, the NTS handed control of sustainable development to the community trust in 2017. Rising to the challenge, locals launched a crowdfunding appeal in 2021 to help raise the funds to build three new family homes – and hopefully double the island's population.

Shops

The Craft Shop & Tea Room

MAP PAGE 52
Port Mór, Muck. www.isleofmuck.com.
The only shop on the island sells handmade crafts, such as garments made from hand-spun wool, mugs and cards with prints and photos of the local scenery. You can also buy food here, with daily soups and sandwiches made from fresh home-baked bread, plus afternoon teas and dinners of shellfish caught along the island's shoreline prepared on request.

Isle of Eigg Shop

MAP PAGE 52
Harbour, Eigg. www.isleofeiggshop.com.
Stock up on island ingredients plus supplies sourced from further afield for preparing meals at self-catering digs or campsites on Eigg. Beer, fish, eggs, fruit and vegetables are delivered most weeks, as well as freshly baked bread. The winter opening hours are more limited

due to fewer ferries and more cancelled crossings.

Rùm Shop and Post Office

MAP PAGE 52
Kinloch Village Hall, Rùm. 01687 460 328, email: rumshop@gmail.com.
Typical of many out-of-the-way places in Scotland, Kinloch has one building that moonlights as the post office, general store and café. Here, you can stock up on essentials for camping or self-catering stays. Specific groceries can be ordered in advance if enough notice is given.

Cafés and restaurants

Café Canna

MAP PAGE 52
West Bothy, Canna. www.cafecanna.co.uk.
Café Canna treats its small community – and passing visitors – to an inventive menu drawing on the bounty of the land and sea. Think kelp-wrapped mackerel with

Fresh seafood abounds at *The Craft Shop & Tea Room*

The view from *Café Canna*

rhubarb or straight-off-the-boat Canna lobster. The team bakes its own bread, forages seaweed from local shores for recipes and pours pints of pale ale from Canna's very own microbrewery.

Ivy Cottage

MAP PAGE 52
Kinloch, Rùm. Email: fliss@isleofrum.com,
www.ivycottageisleofrum.co.uk.
Ivy Cottage is helmed by welcoming owners who are known to make a fine meal. While the husband-and-wife team usually prepare dinners for guests (included in the price of a stay), they will also try to cater to non-residents who email in advance. Meals are vegetarian and vegan, and there are loch views from the dining space.

Kim's Kitchen

MAP PAGE 52
Kinloch Village Hall, Rùm.
Email: isleofrumteashop@gmail.com.
Located in the Rùm village hall beside the general store and post office, *Kim's Kitchen* has a range of fresh food – home-made soup, chunky sandwiches, freshly baked banana loaf – and a more formal evening menu. The highlight, though, is the Friday Fish Supper, when catch of the day is fried in Prosecco batter to eat in or take away. Send an email in advance of your visit as ingredients are ordered based on anticipated demand.

Bar

Galmisdale Bay

MAP PAGE 52
Galmisdale, Eigg. www.galmisdale-bay.com.
The outdoor terrace at Eigg's premier watering hole is the place to be on a sunny afternoon, sipping on a draught beer produced by the island's very own Laig Bay Brewing Company. Stay long enough for decent pub grub – think steak pie or fish and chips – and perhaps some live music when the bar livens up after dark.

THE WESTERN ISLES

The Western Isles (also known as the Outer Hebrides) form a 130-mile-long archipelago, stretching from Lewis and Harris in the north to the Uists and Barra in the south. The islands appear as an unbroken chain when viewed from across the Minch, hence their nickname, the Long Isle. In reality, there are more than two hundred islands, although only a handful are inhabited, with the total combined population nudging 27,000. This is truly a land on the edge, where the turbulent seas of the Atlantic smash up against a geologically complex terrain, whose coastline is gouged by a thousand sheltered bays and laced by sweeping sandy beaches. The islands' interiors are equally dramatic, veering from looming mountaintops to flat, loch-studded lunar landscapes and treeless peat moorland.

Shawbost Norse Mill and Kiln on the Isle of Lewis

View over South Uist from an interisland passenger flight

The major difference between the Western Isles and much of the Hebrides is that the islands' fragile economy is still mainly concentrated around crofting, fishing and weaving, and the number of migrants to the islands is low. In fact, the Outer Hebrides remain the heartland of **Gaelic culture**. The language is spoken by the majority of islanders; its survival partly thanks to the efforts of the Western Islands Council, the Scottish parliament and the influence of the Church in the region – the Free Church and its offshoots in Lewis, Harris and North Uist, and the Catholic Church in South Uist and Barra.

Lewis and Harris form two parts of the same island. The interior of the northernmost, **Lewis**, is mostly peat moor, a barren and marshy tract that gives way to the bare peaks of **North Harris**. Across a narrow isthmus lies **South Harris**, with wide beaches of golden sand trimming the Atlantic in full view of the rough boulder-strewn mountains to the east. Across the Sound of Harris, to the south, a string of tiny, flatter isles linked by causeways – **North Uist**, **Benbecula** and **South Uist** – offers breezy beaches, whose fine sands front a narrow band of boggy farmland and machair grassland which, in turn, is bordered by a lower range of hills to the east. Finally, tiny **Barra** contains all the above landscapes in one small Hebridean package.

Baleshare is a flat tidal island

Lewis (Leodhas)

Shaped rather like the top of an ice-cream cone, Lewis is the largest and most populous of the Western Isles. Nearly half of the island's inhabitants live in the crofting and fishing villages strung along the northwest coast, between Callanish (Calanais) and Port of Ness (Port Nis), in one of the country's most densely populated rural areas. On this coast, you'll also find the best-preserved prehistoric remains – Dun Carloway (Dùn Charlabhaigh) and the Callanish standing stones. The landscape is mostly peat bog – hence the island's Gaelic name, from *leogach* (marshy) – but the shoreline is more dramatic, especially around the Butt of Lewis, the island's northernmost tip. The rest of the population live in Stornoway, on the east coast, the only real town in the Western Isles. To the south, where Lewis is physically connected to Harris, the land rises to over 1800ft, providing an exhilarating backdrop for the excellent beaches that pepper the isolated western coastline around Uig.

Stornoway (Steòrnabhagh)

MAP PAGE 64

In these parts, **Stornoway** is a buzzing metropolis, and with around six thousand inhabitants is the biggest settlement in Skye and the Western Isles.

It's a centre for employment, a social hub for the island and home to the Western Isles Council, or Comhairle nan Eilean Siar, set up in 1974, which has done so much to promote Gaelic language and culture. Aesthetics are not the town's strong point, however, and the urban pleasures on offer are limited, but in July, Stornoway hosts HebCelt (www.hebceltfest.com), a Celtic music festival held in the grounds of **Lews Castle** and at **An Lanntair arts centre**.

Stornoway Harbour

Stornoway Harbour

MAP PAGE 64

For centuries, life in Stornoway has focused on its thriving **harbour**, whose quayside was once filled with wooden barrels of pickled herring, and whose deep and sheltered waters were thronged with coastal steamers and traditional fishing boats in their nineteenth-century heyday, when over a thousand vessels were based at the port.

Today, most of the catch is landed on the mainland, and, despite the daily comings and goings of the tourist-carting CalMac ferry from Ullapool, the harbour is sadly a shadow of its former commercial self.

The nicest section is Cromwell Street Quay, by the tourist office, where the remaining fishing fleet is moored for the night.

Stornoway Town Hall

MAP PAGE 64
20 South Beach.

Stornoway's commercial centre, to the east of the town, is little more than a string of unprepossessing shops and local bars. The one exception is the old **Town Hall** situated on South Beach, a splendid Scots Baronial building from 1905, its rooftop peppered with conical towers, above which a central clocktower rises. It occasionally hosts arts and cultural events so check before your trip.

Harris Tweed

Far from being a picturesque cottage industry, as it's sometimes presented, the production of Harris Tweed is vital to the local economy, with a well-organized and unionized workforce. Traditionally, the tweed was made by women, from the wool of their own sheep, to provide clothing for their families, using a 2500-year-old process. Each woman was responsible for plucking the wool by hand, washing and scouring it, dyeing it with lichen, heather flowers or ragwort, carding (smoothing and straightening the wool, often adding butter to grease it), spinning and weaving. Finally, the cloth was dipped in stale urine and "waulked" by a group of women, who beat the cloth on a table to soften and shrink it while singing Gaelic waulking songs. Harris Tweed was originally made all over the islands, and was known simply as clò mór (big cloth).

In the mid-nineteenth century, Catherine Murray, **Countess of Dunmore**, who owned a large part of Harris, started to sell surplus cloth to her aristocratic friends; she then sent two sisters from Strond (Srannda) to Paisley to learn the trade. On their return, they formed the genesis of the modern industry, which continues to serve as a vital source of work for islanders, though demand (and therefore employment levels) can fluctuate wildly as fashions change.

To earn the official **Harris Tweed Authority** (HTA) trademark of the **Orb** and the Maltese Cross – taken from Lady Dunmore's coat of arms – the fabric has to be handwoven on the Outer Hebrides from 100 percent pure new Scottish wool, while the other parts of the manufacturing process must take place only in the local mills.

The main **mills** are in Carloway and Shawbost, in Lewis, where the wool is dyed, carded and spun. The past few decades have witnessed a revival of traditional tweed-making techniques, with several small producers following old methods, using indigenous plants and bushes to **dye** the cloth: yellow comes from rocket and broom; green from heather; grey and black from iris and oak; and, most popular of all, reddish brown from crotal, a flat grey lichen scraped off rocks.

LEWIS (LEODHAS)

Harris Tweed Authority

MAP PAGE 64

20 South Beach, Town Hall, Stornoway. www.harristweed.org. Charge.

On the first floor of the Town Hall is the statutory body responsible for maintaining the authenticity of Harris Tweed cloth, as well as promoting it around the world. Look for the Maltese cross-topped orb stamp that is pressed onto every bit of cloth deemed to pass muster. Within the building, you can visit the Story Room, a fascinating exhibition tracing the history and culture of Harris Tweed and exploring the production process from wool to weave to wear. Check online for upcoming live weaving demonstrations, which usually take place in the early afternoon of Thursday and Friday during the summer. You can also find out about other tweed workshops that are open across the island here.

An Lanntair arts centre

MAP PAGE 64

Kenneth St. www.lanntair.com.

One block east along South Beach from the Town Hall, and looking rather like a modern church, you'll find **An Lanntair** (Gaelic for "lantern"), Stornoway's modern cultural hub. Films, live music, comedy nights and theatre all take place here, along with poetry readings, talks and all manner of other creative and cultural events. The centre hosts the annual HebCelt festival in July, providing a stage for musicians and bands. There's also a programme of regular creative workshops.

Lews Castle

MAP PAGE 64

Across the bay from the town centre. www.lews-castle.co.uk. Free.

The castellated pomposity of **Lews Castle** was built by Sir James Matheson in 1863 after resettling

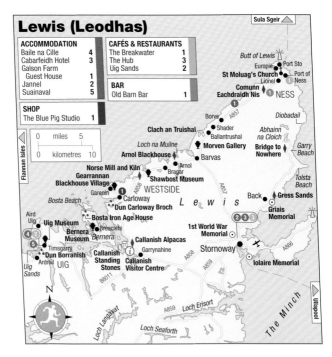

Lewis (Leodhas)

Sula Sgeir △

ACCOMMODATION
Baile na Cille	4
Cabarfeidh Hotel	3
Galson Farm	
Guest House	1
Jannel	2
Suainaval	5

CAFÉS & RESTAURANTS
The Breakwater	1
The Hub	3
Uig Sands	2

BAR
Old Barn Bar	1

SHOP
The Blue Pig Studio	1

0 miles 5
0 kilometres 10

Flannan Isles

Butt of Lewis
Europie • Port Sto
St Moluag's Church • Lionel • Port of Ness
Comunn Eachdraidh Nis • NESS
Borve
Diobadail
Clach an Truishal • Shader
Ballantrushal • Morven Gallery
Abhainn na Cloich
Bridge to Nowhere
Garry Beach
Arnol Blackhouse • Arnol
Barvas
Norse Mill and Kiln • Bragar
Gearrannan • Shawbost Museum
Blackhouse Village
Tolsta Beach
Garenin • Carloway • WESTSIDE
Bosta Beach
Dun Carloway Broch • Back
Gress Sands
Aird Uig
Uig Museum • Bosta Iron Age House
Breaclete • Griais Memorial
Bernera Museum • Bernera
Callanish Alpacas
1st World War Memorial
Timsgarry • Garrynahine
Dun Borranish • Callanish Standing Stones • Callanish Visitor Centre
Stornoway
Ardroil • UIG
Iolaire Memorial
Uig Sands
L e w i s
A857
A858
A859
A866
A867
B8011
Loch Langavat
Loch Erisort
Loch Seaforth
The Minch
Ullapool
N

the crofters who used to live here. As the former laird's pad, it has long been seen by many as a symbol of old oppression: it was here, in the house's now-defunct conservatory, that Lady Matheson famously gave tea to the Bernera protesters, when they marched on Stornoway prior to rioting. When the eccentric Lord Leverhulme took up residence, he had unglazed bedroom windows which allowed the wind and rain to enter, and gutters in the asphalt floor to carry off the residue.

After falling empty for 25 years, the building underwent a £19.5 million regeneration and reopened in 2016, with the restored ballroom, dining room, library and morning room open to the public. A shiny extension houses the bilingual **Museum**

Lews Castle

The Iolaire disaster

Of the 6200 men from the Western Isles who served in World War I, around a thousand died. It was the highest casualty rate per capita in the British Empire. Yet, on New Year's Day 1919, in the single most terrible tragedy to befall Lewis, another 208 perished. Some 530 servicemen were gathered at Kyle of Lochalsh to return home to Lewis on the mailboat. As there were so many of them, an extra boat was called into service, HMY *Iolaire*, originally built as a luxury yacht in 1881. The boat left at 7.30pm heavily overloaded, carrying 284 young men and veterans, friends and relatives, to cross the Minch. In the early hours of the morning as the boat approached Stornoway harbour, it struck a group of rocks called Blastan Thuilm (Beasts of Holm). In the darkness, it was impossible for those on board to see that they were in fact only twenty yards from the shore.

One man, a boatbuilder from Ness (Nis), a village that was to lose 21 men that night, fought his way ashore with a lifeline which saved the lives of forty others. Another was saved by clinging to the mast for seven hours, but he lost his elder brother, who'd postponed his return so that they could come back together. Another man, when on active service, had spent 36 hours in the sea, the sole survivor of his torpedoed ship; now he drowned within sight of his home. Every village in Lewis lost at least one returning loved one, and this, together with the losses in the war and the mass emigration that followed, cast a shadow over life on Lewis for decades. It was the worst peacetime shipping disaster in home waters that century. The ship's bell is in the Museum nan Eilean in Stornoway (see page 64).

nan Eilean, which tells the story of the islands' geology, Gaelic culture, and struggles of the nineteenth century and the Leverhulme era. Six of the twelfth-century Lewis Chessmen from the British Museum collection are on display in the permanent exhibition.

The upper floors of the castle have been repurposed as a clutch of self-catering apartments and suites for those who want to sleep like nobility for the night. In 2019, the hefty restorations were recognized when the castle made it through to the final of the Channel 4 *Great British Buildings Restoration*, and was awarded joint winner in the Victorian category of the competition.

Lews Castle's external attraction is its mature wooded **grounds**, a unique sight on the Western Isles, for which Matheson imported thousands of tons of soil. Hidden among the trees is the **Woodland Centre**, which has a straightforward exhibition on the history of the castle and the island, and a decent café serving soup, salads and cakes.

Iolaire Memorial

MAP PAGE 62

A solemn stone memorial looking out over the Minch to commemorate the 208 lives that were tragically lost close to shore here following a shipwreck on New Year's Day 1919 (see page 63).

Back (Am Bac)

MAP PAGE 62
Bus #W5 from Stornoway.
The dead-end B895 that runs along Lewis's scenic east coast, north of Stornoway – an area known as **Back** – is laced by golden beaches and marks the starting point of a lovely coastal walk to Ness.

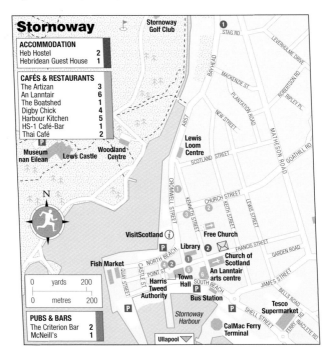

Stornoway

ACCOMMODATION	
Heb Hostel	2
Hebridean Guest House	1

CAFÉS & RESTAURANTS	
The Artizan	3
An Lanntair	6
The Boatshed	1
Digby Chick	4
Harbour Kitchen	5
HS-1 Café-Bar	1
Thai Café	2

PUBS & BARS	
The Criterion Bar	2
McNeill's	1

Stornoway Golf Club

STAG RD
LEVERHULME DRIVE
BAYHEAD
MACKENZIE ST
ROBERTSON RD
RIPLEY PL
PLANTATION ROAD
NEW STREET
A857
MATHESON ROAD
GOATHILL RD

Museum nan Eilean   Lews Castle   Woodland Centre

Lewis Loom Centre
SCOTLAND STREET

CROMWELL STREET
KENNETH STREET
CHURCH STREET
KEITH STREET
LEWIS STREET

VisitScotland (i)   Free Church

Library   Church of Scotland

FRANCIS STREET
GARDEN ROAD

Fish Market

NORTH BEACH
POINT ST
CASTLE ST
QUAY STREET

An Lanntair arts centre

Harris Tweed Authority   Town Hall   SOUTH BEACH

Bus Station

JAMES STREET
BELLS ROAD

Stornoway Harbour

CalMac Ferry Terminal

Tesco Supermarket

SHELL STREET
FERRY ROAD
INACLETE RD

N

| 0 | yards | 200 |
| 0 | metres | 200 |

Ullapool ▽

The Bridge to Nowhere

Griais Memorial

MAP PAGE 62
Bus #W5 from Stornoway.

The legacy of Lord Leverhulme's brief ownership of Lewis is recalled by the striking **Griais Memorial** to the Lewis land-raiders, situated by Griais Bridge, above Gress Sands. It was here that Leverhulme's plans came unstuck: he wanted to turn the surrounding crofting land into three large farms, which would provide milk for the workers of his fish-canning factory; the local crofters just wanted to return to their traditional way of life. Such was Leverhulme's fury at the land-raiders from Gress (Griais) and nearby Coll (Col), a mile to the south, that, when he offered to gift the crofts of Lewis to their owners, he made sure the offer didn't include Gress and Coll. The stone-built memorial is a symbolic croft split asunder by Leverhulme's interventions.

The path to Ness

MAP PAGE 62

Further north, beyond Tolsta (Tolastadh), is the finest of the coast's sandy **beaches**, Garry (Gheardha), and the beginning of the footpath to Ness. Shortly after leaving the bay, the path crosses the **Bridge to Nowhere**, built by Leverhulme as part of an unrealized plan to forge a new road along the east coast to Ness. Evocatively christened for its striking inundation at high tide, the bridge does in fact go somewhere, at least at low tide, when it connects the Biel Water and the beach at Belhaven Bay. When the waters rise around the bridge's steps, though, it's a brain-bending sight, beloved of photographers and locals alike. Further along the track, there's a fine **waterfall** on the River of Stones (Abhainn na Cloich). The makeshift road peters out, but a waymarked path continues for another ten miles via the old sheiling village of **Diobadail**, to Ness (see page 66). It's very boggy, and badly churned up in places, so make sure you've got proper footwear.

The road to Barvas (Barabhas)

MAP PAGE 62

The A857 crosses the vast, barren peat bog (see page 68) that characterizes the interior of Lewis, an empty, undulating wilderness riddled with stretch marks formed

Port of Ness

by peat cuttings and pockmarked with freshwater lochans. The whole area was once covered by forests, but these disappeared long ago, leaving a deposit of peat that continues to serve as a valuable energy source, with each crofter being assigned a slice of the bog.

Barvas

MAP PAGE 62
Bus #W1 from Stornoway.

Twelve miles across the peat bog, the road approaches the west coast of Lewis and divides, heading southwest towards Callanish, or northeast through **Barvas** (Barabhas), which has a handy shop. Three miles further, you pass the 20ft monolith of **Clach an Truiseil**, the first of a series of prehistoric standing stones and other relics between the crofting and weaving settlements of **Ballantrushal** (Baile an Truiseil) and **Shader** (Siadar).

Ness (Nis)

MAP PAGE 62
Bus #W1 from Stornoway.

At the northern tip of Lewis, Ness (Nis) is made up of a string of densely populated, fervently Presbyterian villages. Ness is home to the highest percentage of Gaelic speakers in the whole country (75 percent), but the local residents are perhaps best known for their controversial annual culling of young gannets on Sula Sgeir (see box, page 79).

These scattered settlements have none of the photogenic qualities of Skye's whitewashed villages: the churches are plain and unadorned; the crofters' houses are relatively modern and cloaked in grey pebbledash rendering; the stone cottages and enclosures of their forebears often lie half-abandoned in the front garden: a rusting assortment of discarded cars and broken-down vans, storing peat bags and the like.

The road terminates at the fishing village of **Port of Ness** (Port Nis), with a tiny harbour and lovely golden beach. It's worth noting that there are few shops in these parts, so it's best to stock up in Stornoway before you set out, or at the store where the A857 and A858 meet.

Comunn Eachdraidh Nis

MAP PAGE 62
Cross School, North Dell (Dail bho Thuath),
Cross. Bus #W1 from Stornoway.
www.cenonline.org. Free.

For an insight into the social history of the area, take a look inside **Comunn Eachdraidh Nis** (the Ness Historical Society). The museum, housed in the village school, contains a large collection of photographs, religious artefacts and local antiques as well as a decent World War I exhibition. There's good café here for light lunches.

Europie (Eoropaidh)

MAP PAGE 62
Bus #W1 from Stornoway.

Shortly before you reach Port of Ness, a minor road heads two miles northwest to the hamlet of **Europie** (Eoropaidh; pronounced "Yor-erpee"). By the road junction that leads to the Butt of Lewis stands the simple stone structure of **St Moluag's Church** (Teampull Mholuaidh), amid the runrig fields, now acting as sheep runs. Thought to date from the twelfth century, when the islands were still under Norse rule, but restored in 1912 (and now used once a month by the Scottish Episcopal Church for sung Communion), the church features a strange south chapel with only a squint window connecting it to the nave. In the late seventeenth century, the traveller Martin Martin noted: "They all went to church… and then standing silent for a little time, one of them gave a signal… and immediately all of them went into the fields, where they fell a drinking their ale and spent the remainder of the night in dancing and singing, etc." Church services aren't what they used to be.

Butt of Lewis (Rubha Robhabais)

MAP PAGE 62
From Europie, a narrow road twists to the bleak and blustery northern tip of the island, Rubha Robhabais

– well known to devotees of the BBC *Shipping Forecast* as the **Butt of Lewis** – where a redbrick **lighthouse** sticks up above a series of sheer cliffs and stacks, alive with kittiwakes, fulmars and cormorants, with skuas and gannets feeding offshore; it's a great place for spotting marine mammals. The lighthouse is closed to the public, and there's no way down to the sea, but backtrack half a mile or so, and you'll find a path leading down to the tiny sandy bay of **Port Sto**, a more sheltered spot for a picnic than the Butt itself.

Westside

MAP PAGE 62
Heading southwest from the crossroads near Barvas (see page 66) brings you to the **Westside**. The main road lies a mile or so inland from the coast, but several villages meander down towards the sea. At **Arnol** and **Garenin** (Gearrannan) there are beautifully preserved, traditional-style blackhouses to explore, and, at **Callanish** (Calanais), are the islands' justifiably popular standing stones. At Bragar, the huge **whalebone arch curving** over the entrance to

Butt of Lewis lighthouse

Peat

One of the characteristic features of the landscape of the Highlands and Islands is **peat** (*mòine*). Nowhere is its presence more keenly felt than on Lewis. Virtually the whole interior of the island is made up of one vast blanket bog, scarred with lines of peat banks old and new, while the pungent smell of peat smoke hits you as you pass through the villages. Peat is made up of dead vegetation that has failed to rot completely because the sheer volume of rainfall has caused the soil acidity to reach a level that acts as a preservative. In other words, organic matter – such as sphagnum moss, rushes, sedges and reeds – is dying at a faster rate than it is decomposing. This means, of course, that peat is still (very slowly) forming in certain parts of Scotland, at an inch or less every fifty years. On the (mostly treeless) islands, peat provides an important source of fuel, and the cutting and stacking of peats in the spring is a part of the annual cycle of crofting life. Peat cutting remains embedded in the culture, and is still practised on a large scale, particularly in the Hebrides. It's a social occasion as much as anything else, which heralds the arrival of the warmer, drier days of late spring.

Great pride is taken in the artistry and neatness of the **peat banks and stacks**. In some parts, the peat lies up to 30ft deep, but peat banks are usually only cut to a depth of around 6ft. Once the top layer of turf has been removed, the peat is cut into slabs between two and four peats deep, using a traditional *tairsgeir* (pronounced "tushkar"). Since peat is ninety percent water in its natural state, it has to be carefully "lifted" in order to dry out. Peats tend to be piled up either vertically in "rooks", or crisscrossed in "windows"; either way, the peat will lose three quarters of its water content, and shrink by about a quarter. Many folk wonder how on earth the peat can dry out when it seems to rain the whole time, but the wind helps, and eventually a skin is formed that stops any further water from entering the peats. After three or four weeks, the peats are skilfully "grieved", like the slates on a roof, into round-humped stacks or onto carts that can be brought home. Traditionally, the peat would be carried from the banks by women using "creels", baskets that were strapped on the back. Correctly grieved peats allow the rain to run off, and therefore stay dry for a year or more, piled up outside the croft.

somebody's front garden gives you a vague idea of how big some of these incredible mammals grow.

Arnol Blackhouse

MAP PAGE 62
42 Arnol. Bus #W2 from Stornoway. 01851 710 395. Charge.

In Arnol, the remains of numerous blackhouses lie abandoned by the roadside. One, however, has been very carefully preserved to show exactly how a true **blackhouse**, or *taigh-dubh*, would have been. The dark interior is illuminated and heated by a small peat fire, kept alight in the central hearth of bare earth; smoke drifts up through the thatch, helping to keep out the midges and turning the heathery sods and oat-straw thatch itself into next year's fertilizer. The animals would once have slept in the byre, separated only by a low partition, while potatoes and grain were stored in the adjacent barn. The elderly woman who lived here moved out very reluctantly in 1964, only after the council agreed to build a house with a byre for her animals (the building now houses the ticket office).

Across the road, in stark contrast, is a ruined blackhouse, abandoned in 1920 when the family moved into no. 39, the white house, or *taigh-geal*, next door. A little beyond the blackhouse, a path leads down to **Loch na Muilne**, where you have a good chance of spotting the very rare red-necked phalarope (May–Aug).

Shawbost (Siabost) Museum

MAP PAGE 62
Old School Centre, Shawbost. Bus #W2 from Stornoway. 01851 710 212. Free.
Two miles west of Bragar, at Shawbost (Siabost) – home to one of the main Harris Tweed mills in the Outer Hebrides – there's a tiny **museum** in the Old School Centre, across the road from the new school. The exhibits – most of them donated by locals – include a rare Lewis brick from the short-lived factory set up by Lord Leverhulme.

Norse Mill and Kiln

MAP PAGE 62
Signposted off the A858 outside Shawbost. Bus #W2 from Stornoway. Free.
Just to the west of Shawbost, a sign points to the restored **Norse Mill and Kiln**. From here, it's a ten-minute walk over a small hill to a pair of thatched bothies beside a little stream; the nearer one's the kiln, the further one's the horizontal mill.

Mills and kilns of this kind were common in Lewis up until the 1930s, and despite the name, they are thought to have been introduced here from Ireland as early as the sixth century.

Gearrannan (Garenin) Blackhouse Village

MAP PAGE 62
Garenin. Bus #W2 from Stornoway. www.gearrannan.com. Charge.
In the parish of Carloway (Carlabhagh), with its crofthouses, boulders and hillocks rising out of the peat moor, a mile-long road swerves north to the beautifully remote coastal settlement of Gearrannan. Here, rather than recreate a single museum-piece blackhouse as at Arnol, an ever-growing cluster of thatched crofters' houses – the last of which was abandoned in 1974 – is being restored and put to a variety of uses. As an ensemble, they also give a great impression of what a **Baile Tughaidh**, or blackhouse village, must have been like. The first house you come to houses the ticket office and café. The second house has been restored to roughly the same condition it was in just before it was deserted, so there's electric light but no running water, lino flooring, but a peat fire and box-beds. There's also a foot-pedalled **loom**, used to make Harris Tweed, in the **byre** and a few sheep are

Interior of a blackhouse

even kept inside with their young during lambing season. The third house has interpretive panels and a touchscreen computer tracing the history of the village and the folk who lived there. A handful have been converted into **self-catering** holiday homes and a bunkhouse.

Dun Carloway (Dùn Charlabhaigh)

MAP PAGE 62
Signposted off the A858 southwest of Carloway. Bus #W2 from Stornoway. 01851 710 395.

Just south of Carloway village, **Dun Carloway** (Dùn Charlabhaigh) perches on top of a conspicuous rocky outcrop overlooking the sea. One of Scotland's best-preserved **brochs**, or fortified towers, its dry-stone circular walls reach over 30ft in height on one side. The broch consists of two concentric walls: the inner one perpendicular, the outer one slanting inwards. The two were originally fastened together by roughly hewn flagstones, which also served as lookout galleries that are reached via a narrow stairwell.

The only entrance to the roofless inner yard is through a low doorway set beside a crude and cramped guard cell. As at Callanish, there have been all sorts of theories about the purpose of the brochs, which date from between 100 BC and 100 AD; the most likely explanation is that they were built to provide protection from Roman slave-traders.

Callanish (Calanais) Standing Stones

MAP PAGE 62
Loch Roag. Bus #W2 from Stornoway. www.callanishvisitorcentre.co.uk. Charge for visitor centre.

Peering out over the sheltered, islet-studded waters of Loch Roag (Loch Ròg) on the west coast, are the islands' most dramatic prehistoric ruins, the **Callanish Standing Stones**. These monoliths – nearly fifty slabs of gnarled and finely grained gneiss up to 15ft high – were transported here between 3000 BC and 1500 BC, but their exact function remains a mystery. No one knows for certain why the ground plan resembles a colossal Celtic cross, nor why there's a central burial chamber. It's likely that such a massive endeavour was prompted by the desire to predict the seasonal cycle upon which these early farmers were entirely dependent, and indeed many of the stones are aligned with the positions of the sun and the stars. Whatever the reason for their

Callanish Visitor Centre

existence, there's no denying the powerful primeval presence, not to mention sheer beauty, of the stones.

You can visit the stones at any time, but if you need shelter or some simple sustenance, head to the nearby **Callanish Visitor Centre**, which has a small museum exploring the theories behind the stones. If you want to commune with standing stones in solitude, head for the smaller circles in more natural surroundings a mile or two southeast of Callanish, around Garynahine (Gearraidh na h-Aibhne). For the kids, the **Callanish Alpacas** are an enthralling addition to the barren landscape nearby, with ducks, peacocks, chickens and goats that can be fed at certain times of day.

Bernera

MAP PAGE 62

Dividing Loch Roag (Loch Ròg) in two is the island of Great Bernera, usually referred to simply as **Bernera**. Joined to the mainland since 1953 via a narrow bridge that spans a small sea channel, Bernera is a rocky island, dotted with lochans and fringed by a few small lobster-fishing settlements. Until recently, it was owned by Robin Ian Evelyn Milne Stuart le Comte de la Lanne Mirrlees, Queen Elizabeth II's former herald, who also claimed the title Prince of Incoronata (an area of former Yugoslavia gifted to the count by King Peter II).

Bernera has an important place in Lewis's history due to the Bernera Riot of 1874, when local crofters successfully defied the eviction orders delivered to them by the island landlord Sir James Matheson. In truth, there wasn't much of a riot, but three Bernera men were arrested and charged with assault. The crofters marched on the laird's house, Lews Castle in Stornoway, and demanded an audience with Matheson, who claimed to have no knowledge of what his factor, Donald Munro, was doing. In the

Bernera has a rich heritage

subsequent trial, Munro was exposed as a ruthless tyrant, and the crofters were acquitted. A stone-built cairn now stands as a memorial to the riot, at the crossroads beyond the central settlement of **Breaclete** (Brecleit).

Bernera Museum

MAP PAGE 62
Breaclete Community Centre.
www.berneramuseum.wixsite.com/website. Charge.

Housed in the local community centre, the **Bernera Museum** has a small exhibition on lobster fishing, a mysterious five-thousand-year-old Neolithic stone ball, a room dedicated to an Iron Age village discovered at Bosta and, of course, a genealogy section. Email berneramuseum1@gmail.com in advance if you plan to visit the museum out of season (Oct–April).

Bosta Iron Age House

MAP PAGE 62
Bosta (Bostadh).
www.berneramuseum.wixsite.com. Charge.

Much more interesting than the Bernera Museum is the replica **Iron Age House** that's been built above a precious little bay of golden sand beyond Bosta (Bostadh) cemetery, three miles north of Breaclete; follow the signs "to the shore". In

Sand dunes at Ardroil near Uig

1992, gale-force winds unearthed an entire late Iron Age or Pictish settlement hidden beneath the sand; due to its exposed position, the site has been refilled with sand, and a full-scale mock-up built instead, based on the "jelly baby" houses – named after the shape – that were excavated. Inside, the house is spacious and very dark, lit only by a central hearth and a few chinks of sunlight. Out-of-season visits (Oct– April) can be arranged by emailing berneramuseum1@gmail.com a least a week in advance.

If the weather's fine, climb to the top of the nearby hills for fine views over the forty or so islands scattered across Loch Roag (Loch Ròg).

Uig
MAP PAGE 62
It's a long drive along the B8011 to remote **Uig**, which suffered badly from the Clearances. The landscape here is hillier and more dramatic than elsewhere, a combination of myriad islets, wild cliff scenery and patches of pristine golden sand.

Timsgarry (Timsgearraidh)
MAP PAGE 62
The main road squeezes through the narrow canyon of Glen

Valtos (Glèann Bhaltois) and on to **Timsgarry** (Timsgearraidh), overlooking the yawning **Uig Sands** (Tràigh Uuige), the largest and most prized of all Lewis's golden strands. The best way to reach the beach is from the cemetery car park in Ardroil (Eadar Dha Fhadhail), a couple of miles south of Timsgarry. You'll find the ruins of **Dun Borranish** here, though very little information exists about its past use or origins.

Uig Museum
MAP PAGE 62
Uig Community Centre.
www.ceuig.co.uk. Charge.
A giant wooden statue of one of the **Lewis Chessmen**, which were found in a local sandbank in 1831, heralds the **Uig Museum** in Timsgarry. Inside, you can see some replicas of the twelfth-century Viking chess-pieces, which were carved from walrus ivory and whale teeth and now reside in Edinburgh's Royal Museum of Scotland and Lews Castle's Museum nan Eilean in Stornoway (see page 63). As well as some excellent temporary exhibitions, the museum has bits and bobs from blackhouses. There's also a welcoming **tearoom** attached selling soup, rolls and cakes.

Shop

The Blue Pig Studio

MAP PAGE 62
10 Upper Carloway.
www.bluepigstudio.co.uk.
Out of decay and decline comes the birth of artist Jane Harlington's creative works. Using mixed media including painting, printing and collage, she channels traditional values encountered in crofting and fishing, both of which are in steady decline on the island, into her art. Call in advance (tel: 01851 643225) before visiting as opening hours can be erratic.

Cafés

The Artizan

MAP PAGE 64
12 Church St, Stornoway.
www.artizanjewels.co.uk.
An inviting art gallery, gift shop and coffeehouse hybrid. The ginger and rhubarb cake is legendary in these parts, and there is also a decent breakfast menu filled with the likes of whipped ricotta and crispy maple bacon on sourdough toast. From Thursday to Saturday, cocktails are thrown into the mix, and the cosy space reinvents itself once again into a buzzy evening hangout. ££

The Breakwater

MAP PAGE 62
Port of Ness. 01851 811 011.
A wholly unenticing café from the outside, but things immediately improve when you step inside this curious little haunt and see the views across the bay. Pick from delicious cheese-blistered pizzas, huge plates of haddock and chips, scampi and daily specials like smoked haddock and mussel chowder or lobster bisque mopped up with freshly baked soda bread. Snag one of the window seats for serene views of the harbour. ££

The Hub

MAP PAGE 62
Willowglen Rd, Stornoway.
www.facebook.com/the.hub.cafe.sty.
An unassuming little place that is behind some of the finest coffee in town. A selection of home-made cakes and light bites staves off hunger pains. ££

Restaurants

An Lanntair

MAP PAGE 64
Kenneth St, Stornoway. www.lanntair.com.
Arts venue with a stylish, modern café-bar-restaurant that serves food all day. Light lunches include home-made soup and oven-fresh bread, or more substantial meals include the likes of burgers, fish and chips and pastas. £

The Boatshed

MAP PAGE 64
Cromwell St, Stornoway.
www.facebook.com/boatshedstornoway.
The Boatshed is all about the bounty of the sea, dishing up plump Hebridean langoustines in a pool of chilli-spiked garlic butter,

Tweed wool

tender Leurbost mussels in a white wine sauce, or local monkfish and scallops. There are some meaty options too, such as slow-roasted Dingwall pork belly or Scottish sirloin steak. ££££

Digby Chick

MAP PAGE 64
5 Bank St, Stornoway.
www.digbychick.co.uk.
Smart, modern, buzzy little bistro with a real emphasis on using local, seasonal produce, such as the famous Stornoway black pudding or fillet of Minch hake. Expect an inventive spin on classic dishes, like smoked paprika breaded squid or slow-cooked pig's cheek with curried mash. £££

Harbour Kitchen

MAP PAGE 64
5 Cromwell St, Stornoway.
www.harbour-kitchen.co.uk.
Sea-to-plate cuisine at its finest, with the menu depending on that day's catch. An inventive menu is packed with artfully presented dishes that look as

good as they taste: think torched mackerel, sweet pickled cucumber with kombu and dulce powder; monkfish scampi with wild garlic mayonnaise; or herb-crusted lobster tail and claw in a delicate seafood bisque. £££

HS-1 Café-Bar

MAP PAGE 64
The Royal Hotel, Cromwell St, Stornoway.
www.royalstornoway.co.uk.
One of the best spots in Lewis to devour great seafood, with a relaxed vibe and attentive staff. The menu is packed with everything from Hebridean langoustines to classic fish and chips, while daily changing specials depend on what's been caught that day. £££

Thai Café

MAP PAGE 64
27 Church St, Stornoway. 01851 701 811.
Despite the name, this is actually a restaurant, serving authentic Thai food at wallet-friendly prices. If you like a little spice, order the Jungle Curry – stir-fried beef and peppers in a spicy coconut gravy. No licence

An Lanntair arts centre

McNeill's drinking den

to sell alcohol, so bring your own bottle (£1 corkage fee). £

Uig Sands

MAP PAGE 62

Timsgarry. www.uiglodge.co.uk.

This restaurant-with-rooms is one of the finest places to eat on Lewis, and at the vanguard of the island's emerging gourmet dining scene. With large windows framing views of Uig Bay, there are few better spots to feast on fresh seafood; the menu is determined by what the fishermen bring in that day. Expect dishes like crab claws served with garlicy butter, Hebridean seafood chowder and half lobster salad. £££

Pubs and bars

The Criterion Bar

MAP PAGE 64

32 Point St, Stornoway. 01851 701 990.

A tiny, authentic no-frills Stornoway pub, with regular informal music sessions that can attract anything from a couple of musicians to a quasi-Gaelic orchestra. Unsurprisingly, it can get a little rowdy during the weekends.

McNeill's

MAP PAGE 64

11 Cromwell St, Stornoway. 01851 703 330.

McNeill's pours a great pint of Guinness and the atmosphere is informally cosy, with plush leather seats and wooden barrels repurposed as tables. There's also a decent range of spirits here, as well as the Scottish classic of Tennent's on draught.

Old Barn Bar

MAP PAGE 62

Cross Inn, Cross. www.crossinn.com.

Making good use of an old crofters' barn, the *Old Barn Bar* has tonnes of traditional charm. There's a beer garden for the summer and a cosy fireplace for the rest of the year, with board games, a pool table and a dartboard for entertainment.

Harris (Na Hearadh)

Harris, whose name derives from the Old Norse for "high land", is much hillier, more dramatic and much more immediately appealing than Lewis, its boulder-strewn slopes tumbling to aquamarine bays of dazzling white sand. Despite their aesthetic differences, the pair are, in fact, one island. The "division" between the two is embedded in a historical split in the MacLeod clan, lost in the mists of time. The border was also, somewhat bizarrely, a county boundary until 1975, with Harris lying in Inverness-shire, and Lewis belonging to Ross and Cromarty. Nowadays, the line is rarely marked even on maps; for the record, it comprises Loch Reasort in the west, Loch Seaforth (Loch Shìphoirt) in the east, and the six miles in between. Harris itself is split by a minuscule isthmus: the wild, inhospitable mountains of North Harris giving way to the gentler landscape and sandy shores of South Harris.

Tarbert (An Tairbeart)

MAP PAGE 78

Sheltered in a green valley on the narrow isthmus, **Tarbert (An Tairbeart)** is the largest settlement on Harris and a wonderful place to arrive by boat. The

Highland cows at Hushinish

port's mountainous backdrop is impressive, and the town is attractively laid out on steep terraces sloping up from the dock.

Isle of Harris Distillery

MAP PAGE 78

Tarbert. www.harrisdistillery.com. Charge for tours.

Since opening its doors in 2015, the **Isle of Harris Distillery** has been a most welcome addition to the island, which has been struck by high unemployment and a dwindling population for some time. Isle of Harris Gin, produced here, is making waves across the UK. The concoction uses nine botanicals, including sugar kelp, which is foraged from the local lochs. The whisky is also on its way, already ageing in the barrels. **Tours**, which last around 1hr15min and include tastings, are run on a regular basis and best booked in advance.

Scalpay (Scalpaigh)

MAP PAGE 78

A high-flying, single-track bridge, built in 1997, connects Harris to

Eilean Glas Lighthouse on the Isle of Scalpay

the boat-shaped island of **Scalpay** (Scalpaigh), from the Norse "*skalp-ray*". Scalpay is the place where Bonnie Prince Charlie is thought to have tried unsuccessfully to get a boat to take him back to France after the defeat at Culloden. On a good day, it's a pleasant and fairly easy three-mile hike along the island's north coast to the **Eilean Glas Lighthouse**, which looks out over to Skye. This was the first lighthouse to be erected in Scotland, in 1789, though the present Stevenson-designed granite tower dates from 1824.

North Harris (Ceann a Tuath na Hearadh)

MAP PAGE 78

Mountainous **North Harris** was run like some minor feudal fiefdom until 2003, when the locals managed to buy the land for a knockdown £2 million. If you're travelling from Stornoway on the A859, it's a spectacular introduction to Harris, its bulging, pyramidal mountains of ancient gneiss looming over the dramatic fjord-like **Loch Seaforth** (Loch Shiphoirt). From **Ardvourlie** (Aird a' Mhulaidh), you weave your

way over a boulder-strewn saddle between mighty **Sgaoth Aird** (1829ft) and An Cliseam or **the Clisham** (2619ft), the highest peak in the Western Isles. This bitter terrain, littered with debris left behind by retreating glaciers, offers but the barest of vegetation, with an occasional cluster of crofters' houses sitting in the shadow of pointed peaks, anywhere between 1000ft and 2500ft high.

The road to Hushinish (Huisinis)

MAP PAGE 78

The winding, single-track B887, which clings to the northern shores of West Loch Tarbert (Loch a Siar), gives easy access to the awesome mountain range of the (treeless) Forest of Harris to the north. Immediately as you turn down the B887, you pass through **Bunavoneadar** (Bun Abhàinn Eadarra), where some Norwegians established a short-lived whaling station. The slipways and distinctive redbrick chimney can still be seen. Seven miles on, you'll come to **Amhuinnsuidhe Castle** (pronounced "avan-soo-ee"), designed by David Bryce in

Scottish Baronial style in 1865 for the Earl of Dunmore. The main road takes you right past the front door, much to the annoyance of the castle's successive owners; peer in to see the lovely salmon-leap waterfalls and pristine castle grounds. It's another five miles to the end of the road at the small crofting community of **Hushinish** (Huisinis), where you are rewarded with a south-facing beach of shell sand that looks across Hushinish Bay to South Harris.

Scarp

MAP PAGE 78

A slipway north of Hushinish Bay serves the nearby island of **Scarp**, a hulking mass of rock rising over 1000ft, once home to over two hundred people but abandoned in 1971 (it's now a private holiday hideaway). The most bizarre moment in its history – subject of the 2002 film *The Rocket Post* – was

undoubtedly in 1934, when the German scientist Gerhardt Zucher experimented in sending mail by rocket. Zucher made two attempts at launching his rocket from Scarp, but the letter-laden missile exploded before it got off the ground, and the idea was shelved.

South Harris (Ceann a Deas na Hearadh)

MAP PAGE 78

The mountains of **South Harris** are less dramatic than those in the north, but the scenery is no less attractive. There's a choice of routes from Tarbert to the ferry port of **Leverburgh**, which connects with North Uist: the east coast, known as **The Bays** (Na Baigh), is rugged and seemingly inhospitable, while the **west coast** is endowed with some of the finest stretches of golden sand in the whole of the archipelago, buffeted by the Atlantic winds.

Harris (Na Hearadh)

CAFÉS
Loomshed
  Hebridean Deli 2
Skoon Art Café 4
Temple Harris 3

RESTAURANT
Harris Hotel 1

ACCOMMODATION
Ceol na Mara 2
Harris Hotel 1
Lickisto Blackhouse Camping 3
Old School House 4

PUBS & BARS
Loomshed Hebridean
  Brewery 1
Mote Lounge Bar 2

Offshore islands

Though three men dwell on Flannan Isle
To keep the lamp alight,
As we steer'd under the lee, we caught
No glimmer through the night. Flannan Isle by Wilfred Wilson Gibson
On December 15, 1900, a passing ship reported that the
lighthouse on the **Flannan Isles**, 21 miles west of Aird Uig on
Lewis, was not working. The tower had been built the previous
year by the Stevenson family (including the father and grandfather
of author Robert Louis Stevenson). Gibson's poem goes on
to recount the arrival of the relief boat from Oban on Boxing
Day, whose crew found no trace of the three keepers. More
mysteriously still, a full meal lay untouched on the table, one
chair was knocked over, and only two oilskins were missing.
Subsequent lightkeepers doubtless spent many lonely nights
trying in vain to figure out what happened, until the lighthouse
went automatic in 1971.

Equally famous, but for different reasons, is the tiny island of
Sula Sgeir, also known as "The Rock", 41 miles north of the Butt
of Lewis. Every August, the men of Ness (known as Niseachs) have
set sail from Port of Ness to harvest the young gannets or guga
that nest in their thousands high up on the islet's sea cliffs. It's a
dangerous – and controversial – activity, but boiled gannet and
potato is a popular Lewis delicacy (the harvest is strictly rationed),
and there's no shortage of volunteers for the annual two-week cull.
For the moment, the Niseachs have a licence to harvest up to two
thousand birds, granted by NatureScot which manages the island.

Somewhat incredibly, the island of **Rona** (sometimes referred
to as North Rona), ten miles east of Sula Sgeir, was inhabited
on and off until the nineteenth century, despite being less than a
mile in width, with a population of thirty at one time. The island's
St Ronan's Chapel is one of the oldest Celtic Christian ruins in
the country. St Ronan was, according to legend, the first settler,
moving here in the eighth century with his two sisters, Miriceal
and Brianuil, until one day he turned to Brianuil and said, "My
dear sister, it is yourself that is handsome, what beautiful legs you
have." She apparently replied that it was time for her to leave the
island, and made her way to neighbouring Sula Sgeir where she
was later found dead with a shag's nest in her ribcage. Rona is
now owned by NatureScot and is an important breeding ground
for Leach's storm petrel. Seaflower Skye runs boat trips there as
well as puffin-watching trips to Uig.

Clearly visible from the ferry to Lewis and Harris, the **Shiant
Isles** (www.shiantisles.net), whose name translates as "the
enchanted islands", are cast adrift in the middle of the Minch,
five miles off the east coast of Lewis. Inhabited on and off until
the beginning of the last century, the archipelago was bought
by the author Compton MacKenzie in 1925, and then sold on to
the publisher Nigel Nicolson, whose family still owns them. The
Shiants have wonderful cliffs of fluted basalt columns that shelter
thousands of seabirds, including puffins, in the breeding season.

The Bays (Na Baigh)

MAP PAGE 78

Paradoxically, most people on South Harris live along the harsh eastern coastline of **The Bays** rather than the more fertile western side. But not by choice; they were evicted from their original crofts to make way for sheep-grazing. Despite the uncompromising lunar landscape – mostly bare grey gneiss and heather – the crofters managed to establish "lazybeds" (small, labour-intensive raised plots between the rocks fertilized by seaweed and peat), a few of which are still in use even today. The narrow **sea lochs** provide shelter for fishing boats, while the interior is speckled with freshwater lochans, and the whole coast is served by the endlessly meandering **Bays Road**, often wrongly referred to as the "Golden Road", though this, in fact, was the name given to the sideroad to Scadabay (Scadabhagh), coined by a local councillor who disapproved of the expense.

The west coast

MAP PAGE 78

The main road from Tarbert into South Harris snakes west for ten miles across the boulder-strewn interior to reach the coast. Once you reach the western fringes, a view unfolds of the most stunning beach, the vast golden strand of **Luskentyre** (Tràigh Losgaintir). The best vistas, though, can be found a little further along at **Seilebost**. The road continues above a chain of sweeping sands, backed by rich **machair**, stretching for nine miles along the Atlantic coast. In good weather, the scenery is spectacular, foaming breakers rolling along the golden sands set against the rounded peaks of the mountains to the north and the islet-studded turquoise sea to the west. Even on the dullest day, the sand glows beneath the waves. A short distance out to sea is the island of **Taransay** (Tarasaigh), which once held a population of nearly a hundred residents, but was abandoned as recently as 1974. South of Luskentyre lies **Scarista** (Sgarasta), where one of the first of the brutal Hebridean Clearances took place in 1828, when thirty families were evicted and their homes burnt.

Talla na Mara

MAP PAGE 78

Pairc Niseaboist. www.tallanamara.co.uk.

This architecturally striking community centre – all clean lines,

An abandoned croft on the east coast

The beautiful beach and sand dunes at Luskentyre

glass swathes and acres of local wood – gazes out over the golden sands of Niseaboist Beach. **Talla na Mara** is a cultural hub rooted in place, from an art gallery hosting exhibitions of home-grown artists to a cluster of creative studios and pop-up spaces. Residents include the *Isle of Harris Fine Art*, showcasing original paintings, prints, cards and handcrafted pieces by local artists Owen and Marigold Williams, and *Joceline Hildrey Illustration*, where the namesake artist designs original watercolours, coasters, placemats and more. The on-site restaurant serves brunch, lunch and dinner to patrons, with a side of glorious views over the Sound of Taransay.

Seallam!

MAP PAGE 78
Northton (Taobh Tuath). www.hebridespeople.com. Charge.

There's a wealth of information on local history, geology, flora and fauna at **Seallam!** The purpose-built heritage centre is close to the village of **Northton** (Taobh Tuath), overlooked by the round-topped hill of Chaipabhal at the westernmost tip of South Harris. As well as detailing the area's interesting history of emigration, it's a useful centre for **ancestor-hunters**, and there's a good section on St Kilda (see page 82).

Leverburgh (An t-Ob)

MAP PAGE 78
From Northton, the road veers to the southeast to trim the island's south shore, eventually reaching the sprawling settlement of **Leverburgh** (An t-Ob). Named after Lord Leverhulme, who planned to turn the place into the largest fishing port on the west coast of Scotland, it's the terminal for the CalMac **car ferry** service to Berneray and the Uists. The hour-long journey across the skerry-strewn Sound of Harris is one of Scotland's most tortuous ferry routes, with the ship navigating a series of hidden rocks as if in a slalom. It's also a great crossing for spotting seabirds and sea mammals.

Rodel (Roghadal)

MAP PAGE 78
A mile or so from Renish Point (Rubha Reanais), the southern tip of Harris, is the old port of **Rodel** (Roghadal), where a smattering of picturesque ancient stone houses lies among the hillocks. Down by the old harbour where the ferry from Skye used to arrive, you'll find the former *Rodel Hotel*, a solid, stone-built, historic hotel originally built in 1781.

St Clement's Church (Tur Chliamainn)

MAP PAGE 78
Rodel.
www.historicenvironment.scot. Free; HES.

On top of one of the grassy humps, with sheep grazing in the graveyard, is **St Clement's Church** (Tur Chliamainn), burial place of the MacLeods of Harris and Dunvegan in Skye. Dating from the 1520s – in other words pre-Reformation Scotland, hence the chunky castellated tower (which you can climb) – the church was saved from ruination in the eighteenth century, and fully restored in 1873 by the countess of Dunmore. The bare interior is distinguished by its wall tombs, notably that of the founder, Alasdair Crotach (also known as Alexander MacLeod), whose heavily weathered effigy lies beneath an intriguing backdrop and canopy of sculpted reliefs depicting vernacular and religious scenes. There are elemental representations of, among others, a stag hunt, the Holy Trinity, St Michael and the devil, and an angel weighing the souls of the dead. Look out, too, for the *sheila-na-gig* halfway up the south side of the church tower; unusually, she has a brother displaying his genitalia, below a carving of St Clement on the west face.

St Kilda (Hiort) boat trips

Britain's westernmost island chain is the St Kilda (www.kilda.org.uk) archipelago, forty miles from North Uist. Dominated by Britain's highest cliffs and sea stacks, Hirta, the main island, was occupied until 1930 when the last 36 Gaelic-speaking inhabitants were evacuated at their own request. The island was then bought by the Marquess of Bute, to protect its millions of nesting seabirds. In 1957, having agreed to allow the army to build a missile-tracking radar station here linked to South Uist, the marquess bequeathed the island to the National Trust for Scotland (NTS). St Kilda is one of only a few dozen Unesco World Heritage Sites with a dual status reflecting its natural and cultural significance. Despite its inaccessibility, several thousand visitors make it out here each year; if you get to land, you can browse the museum for an understanding of St Kilda's history, natural wonders and its people. Between mid-May and mid-August, the NTS organizes volunteer **work parties**, which either restore and maintain the old buildings or take part in archeological digs. For more information, contact the NTS (www.nts.org.uk). For the armchair traveller, the best general book on St Kilda is Tom Steel's *The Life and Death of St Kilda*, or else there's the classic 1937 film *The Edge of the World* by Michael Powell (which was actually shot on Foula in Shetland).

Several companies offer **boat day-trips**: Sea Trek (www.seatrek.co.uk) departs from Miavaig (Miabhaig) in Uig for regular jaunts to St Kilda (and occasionally to Sula Sgeir and Rona), as does Kilda Cruises (www.kildacruises.co.uk), which operates a 55ft motor cruiser from West Tarbert on Harris, and also offers charter trips to the likes of the Shiant Isles, Flannan Isles, Rona and the Monach Isles. The sea journey to St Kilda (8hr return) is not for the faint-hearted and there's no guarantee that you'll be able to land. For longer trips around the islands, contact Island Cruising (www.island-cruising.com), based at Miavaig (Miabhaig) in Uig.

Cafés

Loomshed Hebridean Deli

MAP PAGE 78
Main Street, Tarbert.
www.facebook.com/LoomshedBrewery.
The team behind uber-cool craft beer microbrewery Loomshed is back with a hole-in-the-wall deli and speciality coffee shop in Tarbert, stocked with oven-fresh savoury bites like steak-and-ale pies or cheese and onion quiche, sweet treats like lemon drizzle cake, and food and drink souvenirs such as heather honey, hand-roasted coffee beans and – of course – bottles of its very own Poacher pale ale and Iasgair craft lager. £

Skoon Art Café

MAP PAGE 78
Geocrab. www.skoon.com.
There aren't too many places to stop and have a bite to eat along the east coast of South Harris, so *Skoon* is something of a boon. There's always home-made soup and freshly baked bread, along with a selection of tempting sweet treats – chocolate brownies, scones, shortbread and the like. £

Temple Harris

MAP PAGE 78
22 Northton (Taobh Tuath).
www.templeharris.com.
Artisan coffee roastery, café and deli in a hobbity stone and timber building on the water's edge. Stop by for an excellent brew and a baked treat, which might be chocolate cake, machair buns or heather biscotti depending on what's fresh from the oven that day. Later in the day, nab one of the outdoor tables and linger over a Harris gin and tonic overlooking the sea. Be sure to pick up some goodies on the way out, perhaps some wildflower granola or wild whisky marmalade. The team is also behind *The House of Potions*, a cool independent coffee shop by the pier in Leverburgh. £

Restaurant

Harris Hotel

MAP PAGE 78
Scott Rd, Tarbert. www.harrishotel.com.
Just a short stroll from the harbour, Tarbert's longest-established and largest hotel is the place to go for generous plates of locally sourced fish and meats like Highland lamb shanks or Hebridean salmon. £££

Pubs and bars

Loomshed Hebridean Brewery

MAP PAGE 78
Cnoc na Greine, nr. Tarbert.
www.facebook.com/LoomshedBrewery.
It seems like no self-respecting place, even a remote Hebridean island, is complete without its trendy craft beer microbrewery. But Loomshed really is a quality spot, with tasting tours and an excellent taproom serving its craft lager and pale ale.

Mote Lounge Bar

MAP PAGE 78
Hotel Hebrides, Pier Rd.
www.hotel-hebrides.com.
A lively pub located in the *Hotel Hebrides*, just minutes from the Tarbert ferry terminal. Great spot to knock back a local whisky, often to a soundtrack of local live music. Also serves a menu of comforting classics, including loaded pizzas, fish and chips, pies and a decent vegan burger.

Temple Harris

North Uist (Uibhist a Tuath)

Compared to the mountainous scenery of Harris, North Uist – seventeen miles long and thirteen miles wide – is much flatter and for some comes as something of an anti-climax. Over half the surface area is covered by water, creating a distinctive peaty-brown, lochan-studded "drowned landscape". Most visitors come here for the trout- and salmon-fishing and the deerstalking, all of which (along with poaching) are critical to the survival of the island's economy. Others come for the smattering of prehistoric sites, the birds, the otters, or the sheer peace of this windy isle and the solitude of North Uist's vast sandy beaches, which extend – almost without interruption – along the north and west coasts.

Lochmaddy

MAP PAGE 86

Despite being situated on the east coast, some distance away from any beach, the ferry port of **Lochmaddy** – "Loch of the Dogs" – makes a good base for exploring the island. Occupying a narrow, bumpy promontory, overlooked by the brooding mountains of North Lee (Lì a Tuath) and South Lee (Lì a Deas) to the southeast, it's difficult to believe that this sleepy settlement used to be a large herring port as far back as the seventeenth century. While there's not much to see in Lochmaddy itself, there are several prehistoric sites in the surrounding area.

Sunset over Lochmaddy

Foggy morning in Berneray

Taigh Chearsabhagh Museum and Arts Centre

MAP PAGE 86
Lochmaddy. www.taigh-chearsabhagh.
org. Charge.

The only thing to keep you in Lochmaddy is **Taigh Chearsabhagh**, a converted eighteenth-century merchant's house, now home to a community arts centre, with a simple airy café, post office, shop and excellent museum, which puts on some worthwhile exhibitions. Taigh Chearsabhagh was one of the prime movers behind the commissioning of a series of seven sculptures dotted about the Uists. Ask at the arts centre for directions to the ones in and around Lochmaddy, the most interesting of which is the Both nam Faileas (Hut of the Shadow), half a mile or so north of town. The hut is an ingenious dry-stone, turf-roofed camera obscura built by sculptor Chris Drury that projects the nearby land-, sea- and skyscape onto its back wall. Take time to allow your eyes to adjust to the light. On the way back, keep a look out for otters, which love the tidal rapids hereabouts.

Berneray (Bhearnaraigh)

MAP PAGE 86
The ferry service to Harris departs from the southeastern tip of **Berneray**, a low-lying island immediately to the north of North Uist and connected to the latter via a causeway. Two miles by three, with a population of around 140, the small speck has a superb three-mile-long sandy beach on the west and north coast, backed by untamed dunes and machair. The **Nurse's Cottage** (free), just past the harbour, has a small historical display on the island.

North Uist's Neolithic sights

MAP PAGE 86
The most remarkable of North Uist's Neolithic sights is **Barpa Langass**, a huge, chambered burial cairn a short walk from the A867,

seven barren miles southwest
of Lochmaddy. The stones are
visible from the road and, unless
the weather's good, it's not worth
making a closer inspection as the
chamber has collapsed and is now
too dangerous to enter.

A mile further down the A867,
a side road diverts to *Langass
Lodge*. Beside the hotel, a rough
track leads to the small stone
circle of **Pobull Fhinn** (Finn's
People), which enjoys a much more
picturesque location overlooking
a narrow loch. The circle covers a
large area and, although the stones
are not that huge, they occupy an
intriguing amphitheatre cut into
the hillside.

Three miles northwest of
Lochmaddy along the A865,
you'll find **Na Fir Bhreige** (The
Three False Men), three standing
stones which, depending on your
legend, mark the graves of three
spies buried alive or three men

who deserted their wives and were
turned to stone by a witch.

The coastal road to Sollas (Solas)

MAP PAGE 86

In just six miles, the A867 will
whisk you from Lochmaddy to
Clachan via several Neolithic sites
(see page 85), but the A865,
which skirts the northern and
western shoreline of North Uist for
more than thirty miles, takes you
through the most scenic sections of
the island.

Sollas (Solas)

MAP PAGE 86

Once you've left the boggy east
coast and passed the turning to
Berneray and the Harris ferry, the
road reaches the parish of **Sollas**
(Solas), which stands at the centre
of a couple of superb tidal strands
– sea green at high tide, sandy
and golden at low tide – backed

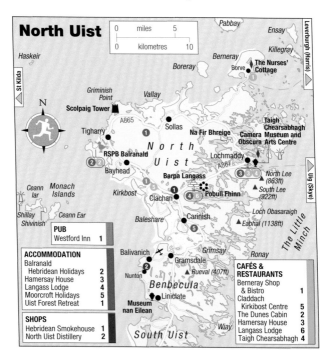

Scolpaig Tower

by large tracts of machair that are blanketed with wildflowers in summer. A memorial opposite the local Co-op recalls the appallingly brutal Clearances undertaken by Lord MacDonald of Sleat in Sollas.

Vallay (Bhalaigh)

MAP PAGE 86

Visible across the nearby sandy swathe is the tidal island of **Vallay** (Bhalaigh), on which stands the ruined mansion of wealthy textile manufacturer and archeologist Erskine Beveridge (cousin of Lord William). Be sure to check the day's tide times before setting out.

Scolpaig Tower and Griminish Point

MAP PAGE 86

Beyond Sollas, the rolling hills that contour the centre of North Uist slope down to the sea. Here, in the northwest corner of the island, you'll find **Scolpaig Tower**, a castellated folly on an islet in Loch Scolpaig, erected as a famine-relief

project in the nineteenth century. You can reach it, with some difficulty, across stepping stones. A tarmac track leads down past the loch and tower to Scolpaig Bay, beyond which unfurls the rocky shoreline of **Griminish Point** (Rubha Griminis), the closest landfall to St Kilda (see page 82). The distant rocky specks are just about visible beyond nearby Haskeir island on the horizon in fine weather, looming like some giant dinosaur's skeleton emerging from the sea.

RSPB Balranald

MAP PAGE 86

Hogha Gearraidh. www.rspb.org.uk.

Roughly three miles south of Scolpaig Tower, through the sand dunes, is the **RSPB Balranald** reserve where, if you're lucky, you might catch a glimpse of the elusive corncrake, once common throughout the British countryside, but now among the country's rarest birds. Unfortunately, the birds are very good at hiding in

Dunlin in the Balranald Nature Reserve

long grass, so you're unlikely to see one; however, you are sure to hear the males' loud "craking" from May to July throughout the Uists and Barra. In fact, there are usually one or two making a racket right outside the RSPB **visitor centre**, from which you can pick up a leaflet outlining a two-hour waymarked walk along the headland. A wonderful carpet of flowers cloaks the machair in summer, and there are usually corn buntings and arctic terns inland, and gannets, Manx shearwaters and skuas out to sea.

Clachan (Clachan na Luib) and around

MAP PAGE 86

Clachan (Clachan na Luib), a small village straddling the main crossroads of the A865 and the A867 from Lochmaddy, has a post office and general store. Offshore, to the southwest, lie two flat, dune-and-machair tidal islands; the largest **Baleshare** (Baile Sear), with its fantastic three-mile-long beach,

is connected by causeway to North Uist. In Gaelic, the island's name means "east village", its twin "west village" having disappeared beneath the sea during a freak storm in the fifteenth or sixteenth century. The tumultuous weather also isolated the **Monach Islands** (also known by their old Norse name of Heisker or Heisgeir in Gaelic), once joined to North Uist at low tide, now eight miles out to sea. The islands were inhabited until the 1930s, when the last remaining families moved to Sollas.

Eabhal

MAP PAGE 86

For a superb overview of North Uist's watery landscape, it's a boggy but relatively straightforward climb up the island's highest hill, **Eabhal** (1138ft). Just north of Clachan, turn right at the signpost for Loch Euphoirt and follow the road to the end. On foot, skirt round the east side of Loch Obasaraigh and approach the summit from the northeast (return trip 3–4hr).

Shops

Hebridean Smokehouse

MAP PAGE 86

Clachan. www.hebrideansmokehouse.com.
Two of North Uist's most abundant
natural resources are put to good use
by the *Hebridean Smokehouse*: peat
and fish. The salmon and sea trout
are caught around the Hebrides,
while the lobster and scallops are
fished around North Uist.

North Uist Distillery

MAP PAGE 86

Benbecula. www.northuistdistillery.com.
Kate MacDonald and Jonny
Ingledew opened the North Uist
Distillery to much buzz in 2017,
and hope to build on the success
of its Downpour gins. The pair
bought an 18th-century steadings
in 2020, transforming it into a
shop, bar and tasting room; the
goal is to create a larger gin and
whisky distillery and offer tours.

Cafés

Berneray Shop & Bistro

MAP PAGE 86

Borve (Borgh), Berneray.
www.bernerayshopandbistro.co.uk.
A useful tearoom and shop near the
ferry terminal, serving breakfast rolls
and farmhouse bread sandwiches,
overflowing with in-season fillings
like Lochmaddy langoustines or
crab mayo. Comforting classics like
cheese toasties and home-made soup
are perfect fodder for nippy days. £

Claddach Kirkibost Centre

MAP PAGE 86

Claddach Kirkibost (Cladach Chireboist).
www.claddach-kirkibost.org.
This community-centre café is in
a light-flooded conservatory with
lovely sea views. Local produce is
used to make soups, sandwiches and
simple dishes, even the occasional
curry or Tex-Mex dish. Cake and
scones are plentiful. £

The Dunes Cabin

MAP PAGE 86

Balranald Hebridean Holidays Campsite.
www.facebook.com/thedunescabin.
After wandering the wind-tousled
RSPB Balranald reserve, there's
nothing better than a piping-hot
scallop and bacon roll from *The
Dunes Cabin*. £

Taigh Chearsabhagh

MAP PAGE 86

Lochmaddy. www.taigh-chearsabhagh.org.
A locals' favourite rustling up
freshly made soups, sandwiches,
toasties and baked goods using
local ingredients from island
suppliers such as the Hebridean
Smokehouse, Charles MacLeod,
and Skydancer, the only coffee
roastery in South Uist. £

Restaurants

Hamersay House

MAP PAGE 86

Lochmaddy. www.hamersayhouse.co.uk.
In one of the region's more
upmarket hotels, this softly lit
brasserie has lots of expensive
seafood options like whole lobster
or langoustines, plus a more wallet-
friendly vegetarian option. ££££

Langass Lodge

MAP PAGE 86

Loch Eport. www.angasslodge.co.uk.
A former hunting lodge at the
edge of a rare pocket of woodland,
mostly serving excellent local fish
and seafood, as well as North Uist
venison burgers. £££

Pub

Westford Inn

MAP PAGE 86

Claddach Kirkibost (Cladach Chireboist).
www.westfordinn.com.
North Uist's only pub – luckily, it's
a good one. An eighteenth-century
factor's house reimagined as a cosy
bar with local ales on tap.

Benbecula (Beinn na Faoghla) and South Uist (Uibhist a Deas)

Blink and you could miss it: the pancake-flat island of Benbecula (put the stress on the second syllable), sandwiched between Protestant North Uist and Catholic South Uist. The only reason to come to Balivanich (Baile a Mhanaich), Benbecula's grim, grey capital, is if you're flying into or out of the city's airport, or you need an ATM or a supermarket. South Uist is the largest and most varied of the southern chain of islands. The west coast boasts some of the region's finest machair and beaches – a necklace of gold and grey sand strung twenty miles from one end to the other – while over to the east, a ridge of high mountains rises to 2034ft at Beinn Mhòr. The Reformation never took a hold in South Uist (or Barra), and the island remains Roman Catholic, as is evident from the various roadside shrines. The only blot on South Uist's landscape is the Royal Artillery missile range, which dominates the northwest corner of the island. Whatever you do, however, don't make the mistake of simply driving down the main A865 road, which runs down the centre of the island, or you'll miss the island's bounty of treasures.

Thatched cottage at Balivanich, Benbecula

Religion in the Western Isles

It's difficult to overestimate the importance of religion in the Western Isles, which are divided – with very little enmity – between the **Catholic** southern isles of Barra and South Uist, and the **Protestant** islands of North Uist, Harris and Lewis. Church attendance is higher than anywhere else in Britain and, in fact, Barra, Eriskay and South Uist are the only pockets of Britain where Catholics are in a majority, and where you'll see statues of the Madonna by the roadside. In the Presbyterian north, the creed of **Sabbatarianism** is strong. Here, Sunday is the Lord's Day, and the whole community (irrespective of their degree of piety) stops work. Shops shutter, pubs call time, garages close, and public transport grinds to a near halt. Visitors should check whether it's possible to arrive at or leave their accommodation on a Sunday, to avoid causing offence.

The main area of division is, paradoxically, within the Protestant Church itself. Scotland's national church, the **Church of Scotland**, is Presbyterian (ruled by the ministers and elders of the church) rather than Episcopal (ruled by bishops). At the time of the main split in the Presbyterian Church – the so-called **1843 Disruption** – a third of its ministers left the Church of Scotland, protesting at a law that allowed landlords to impose ministers against parishioners' wishes, and formed the breakaway **Free Church of Scotland** (whose churches you'll find all around Skye and the Western Isles). These churches are sometimes referred to as the "**Wee Frees**", though this term is also used for members of the Free Presbyterian Church of Scotland. Since those days there have been several amalgamations and reconciliations with the Church of Scotland, as well as further splits.

The various brands and subdivisions of the Presbyterian Church may appear trivial to outsiders, but to the worshippers of Lewis, Harris and North Uist (as well as much of Skye and Raasay) they are still keenly felt. In part, this is due to social and cultural reasons: Free Church elders helped organize resistance to the Clearances, and the Wee Frees have contributed greatly to preserving the **Gaelic language**. A Free Church service is a memorable experience. There's no set service or prayer book and no hymns, only biblical readings, psalm singing and a sermon; the pulpit is the architectural focus of the church, not the altar, and communion is taken only on special occasions. If you want to attend a service, the Free Church on Kenneth Street in Stornoway has one of the UK's largest Sunday-evening congregations, with up to 1500 people attending.

Museum nan Eilean

MAP PAGE 92
Liniclate School (Sgoil Lionacleit), Benbecula. 01870 603 692. Phone to check if there is currently an exhibition running and for opening times.

The only secondary school (and public swimming pool) on the Uists and Benbecula is in Liniclate (Lionacleit), in the south of the island. The school is home to the small **Museum nan Eilean**, which puts on temporary exhibitions on the history of the islands, as well as occasional live music and other cultural events.

Howmore

MAP PAGE 92

The northern half of South Uist contains the best **mountains** and **beaches**. To climb the peaks, you need a detailed 1:25,000 OS map in order to negotiate the island's maze of lochans. To reach the beaches (or even see them), you have to head off the main road and pass through the old crofters' villages that straggle along the west coast. One of the best places to reach the sandy shoreline is at **Howmore** (Tobha Mòr), a pretty little crofting settlement with a clutch of restored houses, many still thatched, including one distinctively roofed in brown heather. It's an easy walk from the village church across the flower-strewn machair to the gorgeous beach. In among the crofts are the shattered, lichen-encrusted remains of no fewer than four medieval churches and chapels, and

a burial ground now harbouring just a few visible scattered graves. The sixteenth-century **Clanranald Stone**, carved with the arms of the clan who ruled over South Uist from 1370 until 1839, used to lie here, but is now displayed in the nearby Kildonan Museum.

Kildonan Museum (Taigh-tasgaidh Chill Donnain)

MAP PAGE 92

5 miles south of Howmore. www.kildonanmuseum.co.uk. Charge.

A reasonably large **museum** featuring mock-ups of Hebridean kitchens through the ages, two lovely box-beds and an impressive selection of old photos, accompanied by an unsentimental yet poetic text on crofting life in the past two centuries. Pride of place goes to the sixteenth-century **Clanranald Stone**, scored with the arms of the clan who controlled South Uist between 1370 and 1839. There's also a 'Feis Room'

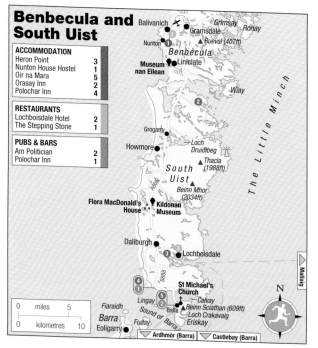

Benbecula and South Uist

ACCOMMODATION	
Heron Point	3
Nunton House Hostel	1
Oir na Mara	5
Orasay Inn	2
Polochar Inn	4

RESTAURANTS	
Lochboisdale Hotel	2
The Stepping Stone	1

PUBS & BARS	
Am Politician	2
Polochar Inn	1

Balivanich
Gramsdale
Grimsay
Ronay
Nunton
Rueval (407ft)
Benbecula
Museum
nan Eilean
Liniclate
Wiay

Grogarry

Howmore
Loch
Druidibeg
Thacla
(1988ft)

*South
Uist*

Beinn Mhor
(2034ft)

Flora MacDonald's
House
Kildonan
Museum

Daliburgh

Lochboisdale

St Michael's
Church
Calvay
Lingay
Fiaraidh
Balla
Beinn Sciathan (609ft)
Loch Crakavaig
Barra
Fuday
Eriskay
Eoligarry

The Little Minch

Mallaig

N

0 miles 5

0 kilometres 10

Sound of Barra

Ardhmòr (Barra) · Castlebay (Barra)

Monument marking the birthplace of Flora MacDonald at Milton

where Gaelic music and culture can be learned and performed. The museum café serves sandwiches and home-made cakes, and has a choice of historical videos for those really wet and windy days.

Flora MacDonald's House

MAP PAGE 92

Follow the sign to "Flora MacDonald's Birthplace", a right turn off the A865 as you head south from Kildonan Museum. This modest monument sits amid the foundations of the home where

the local heroine, who assisted the audacious escape of Bonnie Prince Charlie, was born and raised.

Lochboisdale (Loch Baghasdail) and around

MAP PAGE 92

Lochboisdale (Loch Baghasdail) occupies a narrow, bumpy promontory on the east coast, but, despite being South Uist's chief settlement and ferry port, has only very limited facilities (there's a bank here, but the nearest supermarket is three miles west in Dalabrog).

Whisky galore!

Eriskay's greatest claim to fame came in 1941 when the **SS Politician**, or "Polly" as she's fondly known, sank on her way from Liverpool to Jamaica, along with her cargo of bicycle parts, £3 million in Jamaican currency and 264,000 bottles of whisky, inspiring *Whisky Galore*, Compton MacKenzie's book, and the Ealing comedy (filmed on Barra in 1948 and released as *Tight Little Island* in the US). The real story was somewhat less romantic, especially for the 36 islanders who were charged with illegal possession by the Customs and Excise officers. Nineteen were found guilty and imprisoned in Inverness. The ship's stern used to be seen at low tide, northwest of Calvay Island in the Sound of Eriskay, until the sea finally swallowed it up. One of the original bottles (and other memorabilia) can be viewed at the island's sole pub, local institution *Am Politician*.

Statue of Our Lady of the Isles on South Uist

Eriskay (Eiriosgaigh)

MAP PAGE 92

Famous for its patterned jerseys and a peculiar breed of pony, originally used for carrying peat and seaweed, the barren, hilly island of **Eriskay** has been connected by a causeway to South Uist since 2001. The island, which measures just over two miles by one, and shelters a small fishing community of about 150, makes for an easy day-trip from South Uist. It is laced with white-sand, boulder strewn beaches.

For a small island, Eriskay has had more than its fair share of historical headlines. The island's main beach on the west coast, Coilleag a Phrionnsa (Prince's Cockle Strand), was where **Bonnie Prince Charlie** landed on Scottish soil on July 23, 1745. The sea bindweed that grows here to this day is apocryphally said to have sprung from the seeds Charles brought with him from France. The prince, as yet unaccustomed to hardship, spent his first night in a local blackhouse and ate a couple of flounders, though he apparently ⌐ouldn't take the peat smoke and ⌐ose to sleep sitting up rather than ⌐ure the damp bed.

St Michael's Church

MAP PAGE 92

Near the causeway, Eriskay.

Built in 1903 in a vaguely Spanish style, the Roman Catholic **St Michael's Church** rests on raised ground in the northwest corner of the island, by the causeway. Its most striking features are the bell, which sits outside the church and comes from the World War I battle cruiser *Derfflinger*, the last of the scuttled German fleet to be salvaged from Scapa Flow, and the altar, which is made from the bow of a lifeboat.

Beinn Sciathan (Ben Scrien)

MAP PAGE 92

The **walk** (2hr return from the causeway) up to the island's highest point, **Beinn Sciathan** (609ft), is well worth the effort on a clear day, as you are rewarded with views of the whole island, plus Barra, South Uist, and across the sea to Skye, Rùm, Coll and Tiree. On the way up or down, look out for the diminutive **Eriskay ponies**, which roam freely on the hills but tend to graze around Loch Crakavaig, right in the centre of the island; its only freshwater source.

Restaurants

Lochboisdale Hotel

MAP PAGE 92
Lochboisdale, South Uist.
www.lochboisdale.com.

The town's long-established hotel is a convenient place to shelter with a pint if you're waiting for a ferry; if you have more time, book a table at the excellent restaurant, which serves the likes of langoustines cooked in garlic and white wine, home-made local venison burger, and beer-battered haddock with handcut chips. The team is also more than happy to help arrange fishing trips and wildlife-spotting boat tours. £££

The Stepping Stone

MAP PAGE 92
Balivanich (Baile a Mhanaich), Benbecula.
01870 603 377.

The Stepping Stone is a small, family-run café-restaurant that serves affordable freshly filled sandwiches, home-baked pies and hearty soups at lunchtime and more varied dishes in the evening, such as grilled sole, steak and chips or chicken curry. £

Pubs and bars

Am Politician

MAP PAGE 92
Rubha Ban, Eriskay. 01878 720 246.

The island's purpose-built pub named after the SS *Politician* is unlikely to win any design awards. However, it offers great views out to sea from its conservatory and pub garden, where you can dine on scallops with black pudding as well as the usual pub grub options. There's a decent range of single malts here, as you might expect. Ask to see one of original bottles from the shipwreck, which they usually have on show.

Polochar Inn

MAP PAGE 92
Polochar (Poll a' Charra), South Uist.
www.polocharinn.com.

One of best places to hole up, right on the south coast overlooking the Sound of Barra, and with its own sandy beach close by. The inn's cosy pub is on the ground floor, with the more formal restaurant dishing up a season-driven menu of fresh Uist lobster, local venison and Stornoway black pudding.

South Uist wool

Barra (Barraigh) and Vatersay (Bhatarsaigh)

Four miles wide and eight miles long, the turtle-shaped Barra is the Western Isles in miniature: sandy beaches backed by machair, mountains of Lewisian gneiss, prehistoric ruins, Gaelic culture and a laidback, welcoming population of around 1200. Once a kind of feudal island state, it was ruled over for centuries with relative benevolence by the MacNeils. Unfortunately, the family sold the island in 1838 to Colonel Gordon of Cluny, who had also bought Benbecula, South Uist and Eriskay. The brutal landlord deemed the starving crofters "redundant" and offered to turn Barra into a state penal colony. The government declined, so the colonel called in the police and proceeded with one of the cruellest of the forced Clearances in the Hebrides. In 1937, the 45th chief of the MacNeil clan bought back most of the island, and in 2003 the estate was gifted to the Scottish government.

Castlebay (Bàgh a Chaisteil)

MAP PAGE 98

The only settlement of any size is **Castlebay** (Bàgh a Chaisteil),

Kisimul Castle

which curves around the barren rocky hills of a wide bay on the south side of the island. It's difficult to imagine it now, but the sleepy village was a thriving herring port back in the nineteenth century, with hundreds of boats in the harbour and a cluster of curing and packing factories ashore. Barra's religious allegiance is immediately announced by the large **Catholic church**, Our Lady, Star of the Sea, which overlooks the bay. To underline the point, there's a Madonna and Child on the slopes of **Sheabhal** (1260ft), the largest peak on Barra and a fairly easy hike from the bay.

Kisimul Castle

MAP PAGE 98

Access by ferry from Castle Slip Landing, Castlebay (call for sailing times), weather permitting. www.historicenvironment.scot. Closed for restoration works.

As its name suggests, Castlebay does indeed have a castle in its

Start of the Hebridean Way sign on Vatersay

bay – and a glorious one at that. Cast adrift on a tiny islet, the picturesque medieval fortress of Caisteal Chiosmuil, or **Kisimul Castle**, cuts a lonely figure on the water. The castle burnt down in the eighteenth century, but when the 45th MacNeil chief – conveniently enough, a wealthy American and trained architect – bought the island back in 1937, he set about restoring the edifice. There's nothing much to see inside, but the whole experience is fun; head

The Hebridean Way

Thanks to the excellent infrastructure for such a remote pocket of Britain, the Western Isles are well connected, either by bridge or by car ferries, all the way from Vatersay in the south, to the Butt of Lewis lighthouse at the northern tip of Lewis. Therefore, you can drive the entire length of the archipelago or, if you want to take more time to savour the remarkable countryside in this pristine necklace of islands, while braving the North Atlantic weather, you could tackle the Hebridean Way by bike or on foot. The cycle route measures 185 miles (298km), while the trail for **hikers** shaves off a few corners at 156 miles (252km).

Given that the finest resource of the Western Isles is their natural beauty and isolation, this makes them an excellent choice for outdoor pursuits. The mountainous stretches, followed by long flat machair plains fringed by turquoise seas, are filled with wildlife, which you have a far greater chance of encountering on foot or by bike than in a car or on public transport. For cyclists especially, it is advised to make the trip from south to north on account of the prevailing winds. The general recommendation is to give yourself six days to complete the entire route. For more information, head to www. visitouterhebrides.co.uk.

for reopening; check the website for up-to-date information.

Dualchas

MAP PAGE 98
The Square. www.isleofbarra.com. Charge.
The Barra Heritage Centre, known as **Dualchas** (Gaelic for Heritage), is on the road that leads west out of town. It's an unpretentious little museum, housing the odd treasure like the monstrance from St Barr's Church in Northbay. There are lots of old newspapers, photo archives and local memoirs to trawl through; the museum also has a handy café serving soup, toasties and cakes.

The North

MAP PAGE 98
If you head to the northern corner of the island from Castlebay, you have a choice of taking the west- or the east-coast road. The west-coast road takes in the island's finest sandy beaches, particularly those at

Kayaking off the Isle of Barra

down to the slipway at the bottom of Main Street, where the ferryman will take you over. It is currently closed for restoration works due to safety concerns, with no set date

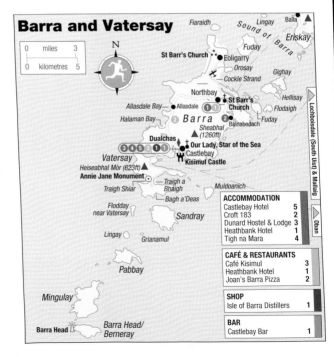

Barra and Vatersay

0 miles 3
0 kilometres 5

N

Fiaraidh
Lingay
Balla
Sound of Barra
Eriskay
Fuday
St Barr's Church
Eoligarry
Orosay
Cockle Strand
Gighay
Northbay
St Barr's Church
Hellisay
Allasdale Bay — Allasdale
Flodaigh
Halaman Bay
Barra
Bàlnabodach
Fuday
Sheabhal (1260ft)
Dualchas
Our Lady, Star of the Sea
Castlebay
Kisimul Castle
Vatersay
Heiseabhal Mòr (623ft)
Annie Jane Monument
Traigh a Bhaigh
Muldoanich
Traigh Shiar
Bàgh a'Deas
Flodday near Vatersay
Sandray
Lingay
Grianamul
Pabbay
Mingulay
Barra Head
Barra Head/ Berneray

Lochboisdale (South Uist) & Mallaig
Oban

ACCOMMODATION
Castlebay Hotel	5
Croft 183	2
Dunard Hostel & Lodge	3
Heathbank Hotel	1
Tigh na Mara	4

CAFÉ & RESTAURANTS
Café Kisimul	3
Heathbank Hotel	1
Joan's Barra Pizza	2

SHOP
Isle of Barra Distillers	1

BAR
Castlebay Bar	1

The boat to Mingulay

A handful of the Bishop's Isles to the south of Vatersay were inhabited until just before World War II. The largest of the islands is **Mingulay** (Miùghlaigh), which once had a population of 160 and, with its large seabird colonies, spectacular sea cliffs and teetering stacks, is often compared to St Kilda (see page 82). The crofters of Mingulay began a series of land raids on Vatersay from 1906, and by 1912 the island had been abandoned, but with none of the same publicity later given to St Kilda. The most southerly of the Western Isles is Berneray (Bearnaraigh) – not to be confused with the Berneray north of North Uist – best known for its lighthouse, **Barra Head**, which rears 620ft above cragged cliffs. Hebridean Sea Tours runs boat trips to the island (www.hebrideanseatours.co.uk).

Halaman Bay and near the village of Allasdale (Allathasdal). The east-coast road wends its way in and out of various rocky bays, one of which, **Northbay** (Bàgh a Tuath), shelters a small fishing fleet and a little island sporting a statue of St Barr, better known as Finbarr, the island's Irish patron saint.

Cockle Strand

MAP PAGE 98

At the northern end of the island, Barra is squeezed between two sandy bays: the dune-backed west side takes the full force of the Atlantic breakers, while the east side crunches with the shell sands of Tràigh Mhòr, better known as **Cockle Strand**. The beach is also used as the island's **airport**, with planes landing and taking off at low tide, since the sandy runway is covered in water when the sea rolls in. As its name suggests, the strand is also famous for its cockles and cockleshells, the latter being used to make harling (the rendering used on most Scottish houses).

Cockle Strand, Barra's airport

Eoligarry (Eòlaigearraidh)

MAP PAGE 98

To the north of the airport is the scattered settlement of **Eoligarry** (Eòlaigearraidh), which boasts several sheltered sandy bays. Here, too, is **St Barr's Church** (Cille-Bharra), burial ground of the MacNeils (and the author Compton MacKenzie). The graveyard lies beside the ruins of a medieval church and two chapels, one of which has been reroofed to provide shelter for several carved medieval gravestones and a replica of an eleventh-century rune-inscribed cross – the original is in the National Museum of Scotland in Edinburgh.

Vatersay (Bhatarsaigh)

MAP PAGE 98
Bus #W33 from Castlebay.

To the south of Barra is the island of **Vatersay** (Bhatarsaigh), shaped rather like an apple core, and since 1991 linked to its neighbour by a causeway, a mile or so southwest of Castlebay. The island is divided into two peninsulas connected by a slender isthmus, whose dunes feature the **Annie Jane Monument**, a granite needle erected to commemorate the 350 emigrants who lost their lives when the *Annie Jane* ran aground off Vatersay in 1853 en route to Canada. The main settlement (also known as Vatersay) has little charm, but it does have a lovely **sandy beach** unfurling to the south; another fine beach, visible from Castlebay, fringes the eastern end of the northern half of the island. Climb up the chief hill, **Heiseabhal Mòr** (623ft), for a wide-open view of the uninhabited islands peppering the sea to the south of Vatersay.

Replica of a rune-inscribed cross in St Barr's Church

Shop

Isle of Barra Distillers

MAP PAGE 98

Castlebay. www.isleofbarradistillers.com.
Founded in 2017, the Isle of Barra
Distillers is the brainchild of local
husband-and-wife team Katie and
Michael Morrison. The distillery's
flagship tipple is its award-
winning Barra Atlantic Gin, whose
seventeen handpicked botanicals,
including carrageen seaweed, are
foraged from the island's shores.
While tours and tastings are not
available, there is a small shop to
pick up a bottle or two. Plans are
underway to move into the whisky
sector, having been given the green
light to build a new £12 million
whisky and gin distillery and visitor
centre, set to complete in 2025.

Café

Café Kisimul

MAP PAGE 98

Castlebay. www.cafekisimul.co.uk.
The family-run *Kisimul* is
something of a local institution
for serving what may well be the
best curry in northwest Scotland.
Dishes are made using super-fresh,
in-season Hebridean produce; try
the scallop pakora starter. There are
good vegetarian options too. £

Restaurants

Heathbank Hotel

MAP PAGE 98

Northbay (Bagh a Tuath).
www.barrahotel.co.uk.
Converted mission church
reimagined as a hotel and
unpretentious local watering hole.
The upmarket restaurant serves
seafood all day; that day's catch
might include Barra langoustines
drenched in garlicky butter, line-
caught halibut or whole lobster.
More meaty mains feature the likes

of wild venison drizzled with a
redcurrant jus. £££

Joan's Barra Pizza

MAP PAGE 98

3 Borve, Barra. www.joansbarrapizza.com.
Filling a much-needed role of pizza
provider to the island of Barra, you
can order takeaway only here and
only over the weekend. While the
leave-them-wanting-more approach
seems to work, make sure you get
your order in as early as possible on
the day to avoid a wait. £

Bar

Castlebay Bar

MAP PAGE 98

Castlebay. www.castlebayhotel.com.
The *Castlebay Hotel*'s bar is wisely
located in a separate building as
this popular drinking den can get
pretty rowdy. This is the best place
to come if you're looking for live
music on most evenings. Soups and
toasties available at lunch, while
the restaurant next door serves
simple dishes drawing fresh island
fare like Barra lamb, local fish and
Hebridean seafood.

Scallops and bacon

ACCOMMODATION

Camping along the coast of Harris

Accommodation

Finding the right accommodation in Skye and the Western Isles often proves to be the trickiest aspect of putting an itinerary together. In the high season, Skye's 'no vacancy' signs rarely seem to get taken down, which means it pays to book a bed for your stay as far in advance as possible. In the Western Isles, while there are plenty of lovely cottages and lodges to rent, part of the challenge is finding somewhere that doesn't require a one-week booking minimum, particularly in high season. In low season, many of the accommodations are closed. Hotels, B&Bs and hostels usually charge by the night, but the range in price varies wildly. There are also plenty of campsites dotted throughout the isles, and a growing crop of cabins, pods and modern bothies. A good alternative for those with a car is to base yourself in one place and then make day-trips. Across this region, most of the accommodation is based in or around the main settlements, but you will also find some wonderfully remote properties with little more than the crashing surf and a craggy outcrop as neighbours.

Skye and Raasay

THE BOSVILLE HOTEL MAP PAGE 26. **Bosville Terrace, Portree. www. bosvillehotel.co.uk.** Central, boutique hotel with twenty sleek, comfortable rooms with vintage furniture and Skye Weavers throws and cushions. Downstairs, the restaurant draws on the natural larder of the sea and landscape, while the exposed-stone bar, with Isle of Skye Brewery ales of tap, is among the finest in town. ££££

THE BRACKEN HIDE MAP PAGE 26. **Struan Road, Portree. www.brackenhide. co.uk.** On the western fringes of Portree, this wilderness lodge turned heads when it opened in 2023. Designed to blend in with the landscape, the stone-built main lodge and 45 wooden cabins are scattered across 52 acres of untamed land. Expect underfloor heating, huge beds and mountain views as standard. Elsewhere, you'll find a whisky room, restaurant, sauna and wild swimming pond. £££

CARTER'S REST MAP PAGE 26. **8/9 Upper Milovaig, 4 miles west of Colbost. www. cartersrestskye.co.uk.** Antique furniture,

Accommodation price codes

Each accommodation reviewed in this Guide is accompanied by a price category, based on the cost of a standard double room (not including breakfast) for two people in high season.

£	under £75
££	£76–£110
£££	£111–£150
££££	over £151

super-king beds dressed with butter-soft linen and a sprinkling of little touches like a digital radio combine to great effect in this luxury four-star B&B. There's an inviting guest lounge with a wood-burner and soul-soothing coast views, and a glass-fronted sauna overlooking Loch Pooltiel. £££

CORUISK HOUSE MAP PAGE 38. **Elgol.** www.coruiskhouse.com. Above the remote Michelin-listed restaurant is a string of four beautiful cottage rooms, with a muted colour palette and vintage one-offs (upgrade to a suite for a freestanding rolltop bathtub). A perfect island getaway exuding understated luxury. Be sure to book a table for dinner to gorge on a four-course field-to-fork feast before stumbling to your marshmallow-soft bed for a good night's kip. Reservations essential. ££££

CUILLIN HILLS HOTEL MAP PAGE 26. **Turn left at end of Bosville Terrace, Portree.** www.cuillinhills-hotel-skye. co.uk. Sheltered among fifteen acres of secluded grounds, Lord MacDonald's old hunting lodge has been reimagined as the smartest formal hotel in Portree: a luxurious country stay with town facilities to hand. The main calling card, though, is the incredible view over the Sound of Raasay. Accommodation is spacious and in a palette of greys, enlivened with splashes of Highlands patterns and textiles. ££££

THE FERRY INN MAP PAGE 26. **On the A87, Uig.** www.theferryinnskye.com. A cluster of just three guest rooms creates an intimate and exclusive vibe at *The Ferry Inn*. Each is individually decorated in country-chic style and comes with a king-size bed adorned with Egyptian cotton linen – the front two have bay views, the back one has woodland views – all above one of Skye's best pubs and restaurants. ££££

GLENBRITTLE CAMPSITE MAP PAGE 38. **End of road, Glenbrittle.** www. dunvegancastle.com/glenbrittle. Wedged between the sea and mountains, just steps from the sands, this spacious, remote site is the best of both worlds. The bad news: midges in the summer – thousands of them, though they vanish with a breeze. The on-site shop and café sells camping essentials and proper coffee. April–Sept. £

GRESHORNISH HOUSE MAP PAGE 26. **Greshornish, 9 miles northeast of Dunvegan.** www.greshornishhouse.com. This wonderful small hotel – half country hotel, half family home – is a remote gem on the Greshornish peninsula. Wild, untamed gardens tumble down to the shores of a loch, where the occasional elusive otter is sighted, while the ten guest rooms are decked out with one-off antiques. Patchy mobile phone signal and limited wi-fi add to the escape-it-all atmosphere that's difficult to leave. No arrivals on Mon. ££££

PORTREE SYHA MAP PAGE 26. **Lisigarry Court, Portree.** www.hostellingscotland. org.uk. Portree's SYHA hostel is one of the best equipped on the island. Some 55 beds across bunk dorms and private doubles with en suites. Dorms £, doubles ££

RAASAY HOUSE MAP PAGE 38. **Short walk from ferry pier.** www.raasay-house. co.uk. The MacLeods' rebuilt manor has been repurposed as a family-friendly hotel with a jam-packed activity programme offering everything from guided walks and archery to canyoning, coasteering and loch kayaking. Spacious rooms sleep up to five, some opening onto balconies framing views of the Cuillins, while the on-site bar-restaurant is the only place dishing up evening meals on Raasay. £££

ROSKHILL HOUSE MAP PAGE 26. **Roskhill, 3 miles south of Dunvegan.** www.roskhillhouse.co.uk. Stone walls, traditional crafts and home-made cake add a huge dollop of charm to this old 1890 crofthouse turned five-room guesthouse. A smattering of modern oak furnishings alongside local artwork hung on walls and bed throws slung over crisp white linen lend understated style to your stay. Great breakfasts too. Closed in winter. £££

SKYEWALKER HOSTEL MAP PAGE 38. **Portnalong, 2 miles north of Carbost.** www.skyewalkerhostel.com. Not just the best hostel on Skye but voted by visitors as Hostelworld's best in Scotland in 2012,

2014–6 and 2019–2020. Housed in a converted school, it's an appealing blend of the practical – solid bunks, and an outstanding kitchen with storage drawers for guests and free tea and coffee – and the charming: pretty vintage-style bathroom, a lounge with wall-hung guitars that hosts the occasional music evening, and a glass garden solar dome peppered with bean bags and cushion-topped benches. A smattering of wooden cabins ("Jedi Huts") has been fitted with double beds for a slice of privacy. Easter–Sept. £

SLIGACHAN HOTEL AND CAMPSITE
MAP PAGE 38. On A87. www.sligachan.
co.uk. A long-standing hikers' institution embraced beneath Cuillin's peaks. Alongside dated but comfy enough en-suite rooms, the barn-like *Seumas' Bar* serves hearty dishes like venison stew, best paired with one of the 400-plus whiskies from the on-site Cuillin Brewery. The campsite is over the road (077 8643 5294). As with everywhere on Skye, the midges in summer are fierce. Hotel: March–Oct; campsite: year-round. Camping £, doubles ££££

VIEWFIELD HOUSE MAP PAGE 26.
Signposted off A87, Portree.
www.viewfieldhouse.com. The last word in Scots Baronial style is this grand pile on the southern edge of Portree. It's almost eccentric in its Victorian grandeur, all fabulous floral wallpaper, hunting trophies, stuffed polecats and antiques. Rooms are individually furnished; some tranquil, some gloriously over the top. The main house is open April to mid-Oct, with two exterior rooms available in winter. ££££

WOODBINE GUEST HOUSE MAP PAGE 26.
Uig. www.woodbineskye.co.uk. This B&B is in a tasteful traditional stone crofthouse on the Duntulm road. All of the five rooms are en suite; ask for one at the front for scenic sea views. The hugely helpful owners also arrange activities, including wildlife-spotting trips and kayak rental.
March–Oct. ££

The Small Isles
THE GLEBE BARN MAP PAGE 52.
Galmisdale. www.glebebarn.co.uk. Eigg's 22-bed hostel on the hill above the harbour has a spacious lounge with awesome coast views and pleasant wee dorm rooms. Better still is the self-contained cottagey *Glebe Apartment* – a superb stay for up to five people. March to early Nov. ££

IVY COTTAGE MAP PAGE 52. Kinloch.
www.ivycottageisleofrum.co.uk. On the shores of the loch in front of the castle, the first B&B on Rùm delivers glittering water views from two pleasant en-suite rooms and the breakfast conservatory. There's a shepherd's hut for self-catering stays too. Its young owners prepare vegetarian and vegan dinners for guests (included in the price) and non-residents on request. Bikes to rent, and a craft shop next door. Rooms ££, shepherd's hut £££

KILDONAN HOUSE MAP PAGE 52. Down a long, unmarked road, north side of Galmisdale Bay. www.kildonanhouseeigg.
co.uk. A traditional stay in an eighteenth-century farmhouse. Warm and welcoming host Marie offers three pleasingly simple pine-panelled rooms, one with an en-suite shower, all with sea views and dinners (usually catch of the day) included. £££

TIGHARD GUEST HOUSE MAP PAGE 52.
www.tighard-isleofcanna.com. The Sanday room is the pick of the bunch – spacious, traditional and with a wood-burner and sweeping sea views – in the only B&B on Canna. Its other two smaller and simpler twins also enjoy sea views. ££££

Lewis
BAILE NA CILLE MAP PAGE 62.
Timsgarry (Timsgearraidh). www.
bailenacille.co.uk. A charmingly chaotic kind of place, run by an eccentric couple who are very welcoming to families and dogs and dish up wonderful set-menu dinners five nights a week for £35 a head (register interest 24hr in advance). The seven en-suite rooms are spread across the main house and converted stable block.
Mid-April to early Oct. £££

CABARFEIDH HOTEL MAP PAGE 62.
Manor Park, Stornoway.
www.cabarfeidh-hotel.co.uk. Large hotel

near Lews Castle with an excellent choice of cooked breakfasts (included in fee) such as kippers, pancakes drizzled with syrup, and the full Scottish fry-up. Also a restaurant with a season-driven menu serving up the likes of Leurbost mussels, Isle of Harris scallops and Scottish braised blade of beef. £££

GALSON FARM GUEST HOUSE MAP PAGE 62. South Galson (Gabhsann Bho), eight miles northeast of Barvas. www.galsonfarm.co.uk. A converted eighteenth-century farmhouse with four bedrooms and two sitting rooms. Friendly owners Elaine and Richard serve up a hearty Scottish breakfast including the famous Stornoway black pudding. £££

HEB HOSTEL MAP PAGE 64. 25 Kenneth St, Stornoway. www.hebhostel.com. A clean, centrally located terrace house painted salmon pink, converted into a simple hostel with dorm-style rooms, double and family rooms, and a shepherd's hut. Rates include a basic self-serve breakfast and wi-fi, while facilities take in a lounge, laundry room, lockers, bikeshed and a fully equipped kitchen. Run by a friendly resident warden. Dorm beds/private rooms £, shepherd's hut ££

HEBRIDEAN GUEST HOUSE MAP PAGE 64. 61 Bayhead St, Stornoway. www. hebridean-guest-house.co.uk. An unassuming whitewashed property, just a 5min walk from the harbour and within easy reach of Lews Castle, with a large range of en-suite rooms and a decent breakfast included. £££

JANNEL MAP PAGE 62. 5 Stewart Drive, Stornoway. www.jannel-stornoway.co.uk. Just a short walk from the town centre, this B&B is run by a delightful landlady, and offers five immaculate en-suite rooms and a good breakfast. ££

SUAINAVAL MAP PAGE 62. 3 Crowlista (Cradhlastadh). www.suainaval.com. The best B&B in the area, run by a warm and welcoming couple; excellent-value rooms have pale birch floors and Harris tweed furnishings and fabulous views over the golden sands of Uig. ££

Harris

COEL NA MARA MAP PAGE 78. 7 Direcleit, Tarbert. www.ceolnamara.com. With your own transport, this secluded four-bedroom B&B, just south of Tarbert, is a good choice. Nicely furnished throughout, with great views over East Loch Tarbert. Breakfast (included) is a bounty of choice; opt for the full Scottish or the local kipper. The smallest and cheapest guest room doesn't have en-suite facilities. £££

HARRIS HOTEL MAP PAGE 78. Scott Rd, Tarbert. www.harrishotel.com. Just a 5min walk from the harbour, this is Tarbert's largest and longest-established hotel. The 23 en-suite rooms are tastefully furnished; the best with sea views. The hotel is open to the public for food – even on a Sunday – with a lunch menu that includes a generously sized venison burger. £££

LICKISTO BLACKHOUSE CAMPING MAP PAGE 78. Lickisto (Liceasto). www.lickistoblackhousecamping.co.uk. Beautiful campsite by a rocky bay with a restored blackhouse for campers' use. A couple of renovated thatched byres shelter basic washing facilities, while the blackhouse is the place to cook, eat and mingle by the peat fire. There is a selection of other accommodation, from an old cattle byre turned snug bothy to a fire-warmed bell tent and a handful of yurts with double beds. March–Oct. Tent pitch/bell tent £, bothy/yurts ££

OLD SCHOOL HOUSE MAP PAGE 78. Finsbay (Fionnsbhagh). www.theoldschoolhousefinsbay. com. Attractive Victorian former village schoolhouse with two en-suite twin rooms. It's run by a very friendly couple who provide good home cooking, drawing on local island produce and vegetables from their kitchen-garden, and generous portions for dinner (extra charge) and breakfast. £

North Uist, Benbecula and South Uist

BALRANALD HEBRIDEAN HOLIDAYS MAP PAGE 86. Balranald. www.

Wild camping

Since the 2005 Scottish Outdoor Access Code was brought in, there has been clarity on where you can and can't pitch a tent. The beauty of this law is that you are allowed to camp out and wake up in some of Scotland's most spectacular places, free of charge. But with this right comes a responsibility too. Don't camp close to buildings or roads, or in any kind of working field with crops or livestock. And naturally, all litter should be taken away with you, without exception. You must also remove traces of campfires and campsites as best you can before leaving. Another thing to consider is the midges. They can make life miserable in summer, so come prepared. The weather in these parts is quite unpredictable, so sturdy outdoor wear and waterproof tents are preferable, if not necessary. Some of the best spots to camp are: Vatersay Bay, near the stunning beach; inland on the Trotternish peninsula; along Glen Sligachan in the Cuillin; and Kilmory Bay on Rùm. It's always best to check locally before heading out that the place you plan to camp isn't off-limits.

balranaldhebrideanholidays.com. Lovely campsite by the RSPB reserve, surrounded by fields of wildflowers and close to a sandy beach. There's free wi-fi, a washing machine and tumble drier, and the office sells basic provisions. March–Sept. Tent pitch £

HAMERSAY HOUSE MAP PAGE 86. Lochmaddy. www.hamersayhouse.co.uk. Eight en-suite rooms with nautical accents, alongside an inviting brasserie with a seafood-leaning menu. £££

HERON POINT MAP PAGE 92. Lochboisdale. www.heronpoint.co.uk. Homely B&B located just a mile up the road from the ferry terminal, with a cluster of four en-suite bedrooms. Efficiently run by a very friendly host who cooks up a wonderful breakfast of smoked salmon and poached eggs. ££

LANGASS LODGE MAP PAGE 86. Loch Eport, just off the A867. www.langasslodge.co.uk. A former hunting lodge located beside a small pocket of woodland – a very rare sight in the barren Uists – and on the shores of Loch Eport. Expect spacious Hebridean-influenced guest rooms, a cosy bar and a decent restaurant showcasing the bounty of the sea and land. £££

MOORCROFT HOLIDAYS MAP PAGE 86. 17 Carinish (Cairinis). www.moorcroftholidays.co.uk. An exposed but flat and very well-equipped campsite with sublime sea views. For those who prefer a roof over their heads, the bunkhouse is pretty luxurious with three twin rooms, acres of pale wood and exposed stone, a modern kitchen and a homely fire-warmed living/dining room. If you prefer privacy, pick a cheery little "hobbit home" with twinkling fairy lights, twin beds, fridge and microwave. April–Oct. £

NUNTON HOUSE HOSTEL MAP PAGE 92. Nunton. www.nuntonhousehostel.com. Four small dorm rooms in the eighteenth-century former clan chief's house, where Bonnie Prince Charlie dressed up in drag before his escape over the sea to Skye. Sadly, the prince wouldn't recognize the place these days as all the charm has been modernized out of it, save for the delightful fireplace hearth. £

OIR NA MARA MAP PAGE 92. 01878 720 216. This unassuming bungalow B&B is maintained by a true perfectionist; the rooms are spotlessly clean and the bedding is high quality. Tea and home-made cakes are offered to guests on arrival, and Eriskay's pub is located conveniently nearby for mealtimes. ££

ORASAY INN MAP PAGE 92. Lochcarnan (Loch a' Charnain). www.orasayinn. co.uk. A modern purpose-built hotel and restaurant off the main road with well-kept, if old-fashioned, rooms, some of which have a private decked area. A good base from which to take day-trips to the Uists and surrounding islands. £££

POLOCHAR INN MAP PAGE 92. Polochar (Poll a' Charra). www.polocharinn.com. One of best places to hole up, right on the south coast overlooking the Sound of Barra. With its own sandy beach close by, the *Polochar Inn* has a clutch of sea-view rooms located above a ground-floor pub and restaurant. £££

UIST FOREST RETREAT MAP PAGE 86. North Uist, HS6 5BY. www.uistforestretreat. co.uk. A trio of wooden cabins perched on stilts among the treetops of a rare forest canopy on North Uist. Each sleeping two guests, these romantic hideaways offer a slice of understated luxury: wood-burning stoves, freestanding baths, cloud-like beds. Large wraparound windows frame views of the woodland and sea. Minimum three-night stay. ££££

Barra

CASTLEBAY HOTEL MAP PAGE 98. Castlebay. www.castlebayhotel.com. The *Castlebay* is the more welcoming of the town's two hotels – a solid Victorian pile, with spectacular views over the bay from the excellent restaurant and some of the rooms. Book way in advance to snag the cheapest digs. ££

CROFT 183 MAP PAGE 98. Balnabodach (Buaile nam Bodach). www.croft183.com. A well-equipped campsite on the rocky eastern side of the island, with a kitchen and laundry facilities. Also a guesthouse with five en-suite rooms, including two family options; a self-catering two-bedroom cottage; and a yurt sleeping up to four. Camping/rooms £, cottage ££

DUNARD HOSTEL & LODGE MAP PAGE 98. Castlebay. www.dunardhostel.co.uk. A relaxed, family-run place just west of the ferry terminal in Castlebay, with twins, doubles dorm beds and a family room. There's a well-equipped kitchen, a long dining table and a cosy living room with resident cats snoozing by the fire. Outside, a couple of wooden pods offer the camping vibes – with a slice of luxury (think electric and mattresses rather than torches and sleeping bags tossed on the ground) Also offers a range of guided sea-kayaking trips posted up on the noticeboard. Dorms/doubles/pods £, family room ££

HEATHBANK HOTEL MAP PAGE 98. Northbay (Bagh a Tuath). www.barrahotel. co.uk. This former mission church has been converted into a five-room hotel, unpretentious local watering hole and upmarket restaurant. Situated not too far from Barra airport. £££

TIGH NA MARA MAP PAGE 98. Castlebay. www.tighnamara-barra.co.uk. For value and location – just a few minutes from the pier in Castlebay – you can't beat this simple Victorian five-room guesthouse overlooking the sea. ££

ESSENTIALS

Shetland ponies on South Uist

Arrival

There are only a handful of ways to reach Skye or the Western Isles. Skye is by far the most accessible, thanks to being connected to the mainland by a bridge which provides year-round and uninterrupted access. Ferries ply the waters of the Minch between Skye and the Western Isles. There are also regular flights from the Scottish mainland. But for these remote islands, both forms of transportation depend on good weather in order to run and thus maintain the islands' connection to the outside world.

By plane

The Western Isles have three airports at Stornoway, Benbecula and Barra, which all run flights throughout the year to Glasgow. There are no international flights here so a connection may be necessary. For most, the quickest, easiest and cheapest way to reach Scotland is by plane. Many then hire a car and continue in that manner from the airport. Inverness is the nearest gateway for much of the region, but you'll get a wider selection of international flights to Scotland's Glasgow Airport, from which it is possible to drive to Skye in around 4hr 30min. There are also good train services running to Glasgow and Edinburgh from the rest of mainland Britain if you're looking for a greener way to travel.

With most airlines nowadays, how much you pay depends on how far in advance you book and how much demand there is during that period. That said, it's worth looking out for sales, which often start 10–12 weeks before the departure date.

Stornoway Airport

Located just outside town to the northwest, Stornoway Airport is served by Loganair, which runs flights from Benbecula, Edinburgh, Glasgow, Inverness and London-Southend, although some of these routes run only seasonally. From the airport, you can take bus #W5 into town, which stops on the main road half a mile from the terminal. Stornoway town centre then has other buses that head out to different corners of the island, although many of them only run a few times a day.

Benbecula Airport

Benbecula's airport serves the island and the nearby Uists. There are flights from Glasgow, Inverness and Stornoway only, much of the time only running once a week. There are buses that run from just outside the airport. The #W16 bus heads to Lochmaddy, and they are usually timed to coincide with the flights.

Barra Airport

Certainly the most impressive of the three airports, if not one of the most impressive in the world, the tides determine when Barra airport is in use because the runway lies on a beach to the north of the island. The only route serving Barra is from Glasgow with Loganair. Bus #W32 connects the airport to Castlebay.

By ferry

Despite the road crossing, there are ferries to Armadale from Mallaig on the mainland as well. Skye's main port is at Uig in the north, where car ferries shuttle to and from Tarbert and Lochmaddy in the Western Isles. Caledonian MacBrayne (CalMac; www.calmac.co.uk) runs these routes and its website posts regular updates about the sea conditions and the impact this is having on those routes. There's also a CalMac Service Status

The Explorer bus pass

If you plan to make other long bus journeys in Scotland in a period of up to 16 days, it might be worth looking into buying one of its Explorer Passes, which allow unlimited travel on either three days out of a five-day period (£52), five days of travel out of ten (£79), or eight days in 16 (£106) across its entire network. A popular choice on a longer journey through Scotland may be to arrive in Skye from Glasgow, then move on north towards Loch Ness or Inverness, all of which are covered on this pass.

app with the same information. The Minch can be a little wild and when it is, ferries don't tend to run. It is possible to take bikes and pets on the ferries, and there are cheaper passenger-only tickets too. Although there are usually multiple crossings per day, there is a reduced timetable in the winter months. Ferries also serve the islands from Oban (to Castlebay), Mallaig (to Lochboisdale) and Ullapool (to Stornoway) on the mainland.

By coach

Citylink buses (www.citylink.co.uk) connect Skye to both Inverness and Glasgow. It's usually a five- or six-hour trip to the latter and in the summer, there are occasionally long delays to or from Uig's harbour, where the coach terminates. There are various **discounts** on offer for those with children, those under 26 or over 60, and full-time students (contact Scottish Citylink for more details).

Getting around

There's no escaping the fact that getting around these islands is a time-consuming business: off the main routes, public transport services are few and far between, particularly in the remoter peninsulas of Skye and most regions of the Western Isles. With careful planning, however, you'll have no trouble getting to the main tourist destinations. As such, the best way by far to explore is either by car or, in warmer months, bicycle. And in most parts of Scotland, especially if you take the scenic back roads, the low level of traffic makes driving wonderfully stress-free.

By bus

Local bus services are run by a bewildering array of companies, many of which change routes and timetables frequently. Local tourist offices can provide free timetables or

you can contact **Traveline Scotland** (www.travelinescotland.com), which provides a reliable service both online and by phone. There is also a free app available for download. The main ones operating in Skye are Traveline (www.traveline.info) and Stagecoach (www.stagecoachbus.com). The local government still runs those that serve much of the Western Isles (http://cne-siar.gov.uk/roads-travel-and-parking/public-transport/bus-services/lewis).

By car

In order to **drive** in Scotland, you need a current full driving licence. If you're bringing your own vehicle into the country, you should also carry your vehicle registration, ownership and insurance documents with you at all times. In Scotland, as in the rest of the UK, you **drive on the left**. Speed limits are 20–40mph in built-up areas, 70mph on motorways and dual carriageways (freeways) and 60mph on most other roads.

In Skye and the Western Isles, there are still plenty of **single-track roads** with passing places; in addition to allowing oncoming traffic to pass at these points, you should also let cars behind you overtake. These roads can be frustrating, but take care and stay alert for vehicles coming in the opposite direction, which may have been hidden by bends or dips in the road. In more remote regions, the roads are dotted with sheep, which are entirely oblivious to cars, so slow down and edge your way past; should you kill or injure one, it is your duty to inform the local farmer.

The AA (0800 887 766, www.theaa. com), RAC (0800 828 282, www.rac. co.uk) and Green Flag (0800 510 636, www.greenflag.com) all operate 24-hour **emergency breakdown** services. You may be entitled to free assistance through a reciprocal arrangement with a motoring organization in your home country. If not, you can make use of these emergency services by joining at the roadside, but you will incur a hefty surcharge. In remote areas, you may have a long wait for assistance.

Be aware that a new drink driving limit set in 2014 (50 milligrams of alcohol per 100 millilitres of blood), bringing Scotland in line with much of Europe, means that even one pint of beer or glass of wine could leave you on the wrong side of the law.

Renting a car

Car rental in Scotland is expensive. Most firms charge £30–50 per day, or around £150–200 a week. The major chains are confined mostly to the big cities though, with the closest to Skye located in Glasgow and Inverness. The best deals are usually found in advance, through booking sites such as Auto Europe (www.autoeurope. co.uk). With all car rentals, it's worth checking the terms and conditions carefully; some companies only allow

Useful bus routes

Here are some of the bus routes linking many of the major sights in Skye and the Western Isles.

Skye

#51 – Armadale to Kyle of Lochalsh
#52 – Portree to Ardvasar (for the ferry to Mallaig)
#55 – Portree to Glasnakille (near Elgol)
#56 – Portree to Dunvegan
#57A – Portree around the Trotternish peninsula anti-clockwise
#57C – Portree around the Trotternish peninsula clockwise

The Western Isles

#W1 – Stornoway to Ness for the Butt of Lewis (which requires additional walking to reach)
#W2 – Stornoway to the west coast of Lewis – serving may of the main sights on Lewis
#W5 – Stornoway to Stornoway airport
#W16 – Benbeciula airport to Lochmaddy
#W32 – Barra airport/Eoligarry to Castlebay
#W33 – Castlebay to Vatersay

Island-hopping in the Hebrides

Because CalMac has a virtual monopoly on ferry travel in these parts, you can make significant savings with an **Island Hopscotch** ticket. A number of different routes are covered, and it's an encouragement to delve deeper into the region, while simplifying bookings. There are currently 30 different variations to choose between, 23 of which serve all or parts of Skye and the Western Isles. Visit www.calmac.co.uk/island-hopping for more information.

you to drive a limited number of miles before paying extra.

Automatics are rare at the lower end of the price scale; if you want one, you should book well ahead. **Camper vans** are another option; rates start at around £450 a week in the high season, but you'll save on accommodation (a good option is www.bunkcampers.com, which has depots in London, Glasgow and Edinburgh). Few companies will rent to drivers with less than one year's experience, and most will only rent to people over 21 or 25 and under 70 or 75 years of age.

Fuel in the islands has always been more expensive than elsewhere in Scotland, and especially so over the past decade or so. In March 2023, petrol prices in the UK dropped below £1.50 a litre for the first time since Russia invaded Ukraine in February 2022. At the time of writing, petrol can be found at £1.46 per litre and diesel for £1.67 per litre, though with such a volatile market fuel prices are likely to continue fluctuating wildly.

By ferry

Throughout the Western Isles, the roads, causeways and bridges are so good that there are only two ferries needed to make a trip along the entire length of the archipelago. These are also run by CalMac. Most ferries carry cars and vans, and, if you're driving, the vast majority can – and should – be booked in advance; there's usually a window of four to six months. There's no need to book in advance if you're travelling on foot; simply buy your ticket at the port office or on board.

Directory A-Z

Accessible travel

Access to many public buildings has improved, with legislation ensuring that all new buildings have appropriate facilities for travellers with **disabilities**. Some hotels and a handful of B&Bs have one or two accessible rooms, usually on the ground floor and with step-free showers, grab rails and wider doorways. It's worth keeping in mind, however, that installing ramps, lifts, wide doorways and accessible toilets is impossible in many of Scotland's older and historic buildings.

Most **trains** in Scotland have wheelchair lifts, and assistance is, in theory, available at all manned stations – see www.scotrail.co.uk/plan-your-journey/accessible-travel. Wheelchair-users (alone or with a companion) and blind or partially sighted people (with a companion only) are automatically given thirty to fifty percent reductions on train fares, and people with other disabilities are eligible for the **Disabled Persons Railcard** (£20/year; www.disabledpersons-railcard.co.uk), which gives one-third off most tickets. There are no bus discounts for disabled tourists. **Car rental** firm Avis will fit its cars (generally automatics only) with hand controls for free as long as you give them a few days' notice.

For more information and travel advice, contact the disability charity Capability Scotland (www.capability-scotland.org.uk).

Children

Skye and the Western Isles are superb places for children to visit. Critically, the locals love kids, and you will find that by travelling with children many barriers are immediately broken and people will spoil your kids rotten if you let them. The wilderness is a fascinating place for children: wide open spaces with fantastical natural wonders that stir the imagination. It's also the perfect place to illustrate to young minds the importance of our natural environments and the reasons why they are worth fighting to protect. Additionally, there are many folkloric tales in these parts, like the kelpies. In general, you will find that hotels and restaurants will go out of their way to provide an extra bed or a child's portion.

Cinema

Portree's old Aros Centre is now the Isle of Skye Candle Co. Visitor Centre, though the new owners retained the original cinema (www.lasportrigh.co.uk). Over in Stornoway, An Lanntair (www.lanntair.com) screens regular films. Other than that, cinemas are far and few between.

Costs

The Islands are a relatively **expensive** place to visit, with travel, food and accommodation costs higher than the EU average, though this has been balanced out with a plunging pound in the wake of Brexit. Given Scotland's – and the UK's – unstable political and economic climate, costs are likely to continue fluctuating for the foreseeable future. The minimum expenditure for a couple travelling on public transport, self-catering and camping, is in the region of £45 each a day, rising to around £70 per person a day if you're staying at hostels and eating the odd meal out. Staying at budget B&Bs, eating at unpretentious restaurants and visiting the odd tourist attraction means spending at least £85 each per day. If you're renting a car, staying in comfortable B&Bs or hotels and eating well, you should reckon on at least £100 a day per person in high season.

Crime and emergencies

The **crime rate** in Skye and the Western Isles is very low indeed. Even the largest urban centre, Stornoway, sees very few offences committed. Out on the remoter islands, the situation is often even more tranquil: on an island like Canna, all the crimes in the last few decades can virtually be counted on one hand. Apart from during a fight at a wedding in 2010, the Isle of Muck (population 27) managed 50 years without a single reported crime.

Discounts

Most attractions in Skye and the Western Isles offer **concessions** for senior citizens, the unemployed, full-time students and children under 16, with under-5s being admitted free almost everywhere – proof of eligibility will be required in most cases. Family tickets are often available for those travelling with kids.

Once obtained, **youth/student ID cards** soon pay for themselves in savings. Full-time students are eligible for the International Student Identity

Card or **ISIC** (www.isic.org), which costs around £12 and entitles the bearer to special air, rail and bus fares, and discounts at museums, theatres and other attractions. If you're not a student, but you're 25 or younger, you can get an International Youth Travel Card or **IYTC**, which costs the same as the ISIC and carries the same benefits.

Electricity

The current in Scotland is the **EU standard** of approximately 230v AC. All sockets are designed for British three-pin plugs, which are totally different from the rest of the EU. Adaptors are widely available at airports and electronics stores.

Embassies and consulates

Understandably, there are no consular services in Skye and the Western Isles. Please see Entry Requirements below for visa information.

Emergencies

For **police**, **fire** and **ambulance** services phone 999.

Entry requirements

EU, EEA and Swiss citizens can enter Britain with just a **passport**, for up to six months. Americans, Canadians, Australians, New Zealanders and citizens of many Latin American and Caribbean countries can stay for the same length of time, providing they have a return ticket and proof of adequate funds to cover their stay. Citizens of most other countries require a **visa**, obtainable from the British consulate or mission office in the country of application.

If you visit www.ukvisas.gov.uk, you can download the full range of **application forms** and information leaflets and find out the contact details of your nearest embassy or consulate, as well as the rules regarding visa extensions. In addition, an independent charity, the Immigration Advisory Service or IAS (www.iasservices.org.uk), offers free and confidential advice to anyone applying for entry clearance into the UK.

Health

Pharmacists (known as chemists in Scotland) can dispense only a limited range of drugs without a doctor's prescription. Most pharmacies are open standard shop hours. If your condition is serious enough, you can turn up at the Accident and Emergency (A&E) department of local **hospitals** for complaints that require immediate attention. Obviously, if it's an absolute emergency, you should ring for an ambulance (999). Air ambulances also operate in remote areas. These NHS services are free to all.

Insurance

EU citizens can access reciprocal healthcare in Scotland if they show a valid passport or national ID card and a European Health Insurance Card. However, it's a wise idea to take out **travel insurance** before travelling to cover against theft, loss and illness or injury. For non-EU citizens, it's worth checking whether you are already covered before you buy a new policy. If you need to take out insurance, you might want to consider the travel insurance deal Rough Guides offers.

Internet

Internet cafés are still found occasionally in Skye and the Western Isles, but wi-fi is now the best way to get online, with free networks available at most B&Bs, restaurants and hostels. If you don't have your own smartphone, laptop or tablet, the tourist office should be able to help – sometimes they will have an access point – and public libraries often provide cheap or free access. Network coverage for 4G and 5G is patchy to non-existent in much of Skye and the Western Isles.

Laundry

Coin-operated **laundries** are still found, but are becoming less and less common. A wash followed by a spin or tumble dry typically costs around £5; a "service wash" (having your laundry done for you in a few hours) costs about £2.50 extra. In the more remote areas of Skye and the Western Isles, you'll have to rely on hostel and campsite laundry facilities.

LGBTQ+ travellers

While there's no **LGBTQ+ scene** as such in Skye and the Western Isles, many Scots have a positive – or at least neutral – opinion of LGBTQ+ people, reflected in positive media coverage by the likes of the *Sunday Herald*. In more remote areas, and in particular in those areas where religious observance is high, such as the more Catholic southern region of the Western Isles, attitudes tend to be more conservative, and gay residents are discreet about their sexuality.

Mail

A stamp for a **first-class letter** to anywhere in the British Isles currently costs £1.10 and should arrive the next day; second-class letters cost 68p, taking around three days to reach the recipient. Note that there are now size restrictions: letters over 240 x 165 x 5mm are designated as "Large letters" and are correspondingly more expensive to send. Prices to Europe and the rest of the world vary depending on the size of the item and how quickly you would like it delivered. To get an idea of how much you'll need to spend, or for general postal information, check the Royal Mail website (www.royalmail.com/price-finder).

Note that in many parts of Skye and the Western Isles, there will only be one or two mail collections each day, often at lunchtime or even earlier. **Stamps** can be bought at post office counters or from newsagents, supermarkets and local shops, although they usually only sell books of four or ten stamps.

There is an impressive network of post offices in the remotest parts of the region. In small communities you'll find post office counters operating out of, or doubling up as, a café, general store, shed or even a private house, and these will often keep extremely **restricted hours**. Most, though, are open Monday to Friday 9am–5.30pm and Saturday 9am–12.30pm.

Maps

The most comprehensive maps of Scotland are produced by the **Ordnance Survey** or OS (www.ordnancesurvey.co.uk), renowned for their accuracy and clarity. If you're planning a walk of more than a couple of hours' duration, or intend to walk in the Scottish hills at all, it is strongly recommended that you carry the relevant OS map and familiarize yourself with how to navigate using it. Scotland is covered by 85 maps in the 1:50,000 (pink) **Landranger** series, which show enough detail to be useful for most walkers and cyclists. There's more detail still in the full-colour 1:25,000 (orange) **Explorer** series, which covers Scotland in around 170 maps. All OS maps now also come with a smartphone download. The full Ordnance Survey range is only available at a few big-city stores or online, although in any walking district of Scotland you'll find the relevant maps in local shops or tourist offices.

Virtually every service station in Scotland stocks at least one large-format **road atlas**, covering all of Britain at around three miles to one inch, and generally including larger-scale plans of major towns. For getting between major towns and cities, a sat nav or GPS-enabled smartphone is hard to beat, but you'll have less luck in rural areas, where landmarks and even entire roads can be positioned incorrectly, leading to long and sometimes expensive detours.

Money

The basic unit of **currency** in the UK is the pound sterling (£), divided into 100 pence (p). Coins come in denominations of 1p, 2p, 5p, 10p, 20p, 50p, £1 and £2. Bank of England £5, £10, £20 and £50 banknotes are legal tender in Scotland; in addition, the **Bank of Scotland** (HBOS), the **Royal Bank of Scotland** (RBS) and the **Clydesdale Bank** issue their own banknotes in all the same denominations, plus a £100 note. Royal Bank of Scotland also issues a small amount of £1 notes every year, mostly for posterity. All Scottish notes are legal tender throughout the UK, no matter what shopkeepers south of the border might say. In general, few people use £50 or £100 notes, and shopkeepers are likely to treat them with suspicion; fear of forgeries is widespread. For the most up-to-date exchange rates, check the useful website www.xe.com.

Credit/debit cards are by far the most convenient way to carry your money, and most hotels, shops and restaurants in Scotland accept the major brand cards. In every sizeable town in Scotland, and in some surprisingly small places too, you'll find a branch of at least one of the big Scottish high-street **banks**, usually with an **ATM** attached. However, on some islands, and in remoter parts, you may find there is only a **mobile bank** that runs to a timetable (usually available from the local post office). General **banking hours** are Monday

to Friday from 9am or 9.30am to 4pm or 5pm, though some branches are open until slightly later on Thursdays. Post offices charge **no commission**, have longer opening hours, and are therefore often a good place to change money. Lost or stolen credit/debit cards should be reported to the police and the following numbers: MasterCard 0800 964 767; Visa 0800 891 725 or via your banking app.

Opening hours and public holidays

Traditional **shop hours** in Scotland are Monday to Saturday 9am to 5.30pm or 6pm. In the bigger towns, many places now stay open on Sundays and late at night on Thursdays or Fridays. Large supermarkets typically stay open till 8pm. However, there are also plenty of towns and villages where you'll find very little open on a Sunday, and in the Western Isles in particular, the Sabbath is strictly observed. Many small towns across Skye and the Western Isles also retain an "**early closing day**" – often Wednesday – when shops close at 1pm, and you'll find precious few attractions open outside the tourist season (Easter to Oct), though ruins, parks and gardens are normally accessible year-round. Note that the last entrance can be an hour (or more) before the published closing time.

Phones

Public **payphones** are still occasionally found in Skye and the Western Isles, though with the ubiquity of mobile phones, they're seldom used.

If you're taking your **mobile phone** with you to Scotland, check with your service provider whether your phone will work abroad and what the call charges will be. The cost of calls within the EU has decreased significantly within recent years, and roaming charges were abolished entirely in 2017. Calls to destinations further afield, however, are still unregulated and can be prohibitively expensive. Unless you have a tri-band phone, it's unlikely that a mobile bought for use in the US will work outside the States and vice versa. Mobiles in Australia and New Zealand generally use the same system as the UK so should work fine. All the main UK networks cover Skye and the Western Isles, though you'll still find many places in among the hills or out on the islands where there's **no signal** at all. If you're in a rural area and having trouble with reception, simply ask a local where the strongest signals are found nearby.

Beware of premium-rate numbers, which are common for pre-recorded information services – and usually have the prefix 09.

Post offices

See Mail.

Price codes

Accommodation and restaurant listings throughout this Guide are accompanied by a corresponding price code; see boxes below and on page 104.

Smoking

Smoking is no longer permitted in any public place in Britain, including at bus stops. Most rooms in Skye and the Western Isles will be strictly no smoking, although if you do wish to book a smoking room, it's best to enquire in advance.

Time

Greenwich Mean Time (GMT) – equivalent to Co-ordinated Universal Time (UTC) – is used from the end of October to the end of March; for the rest of the year the country switches to **British Summer Time** (BST), one hour ahead of GMT.

Tipping

There are no fixed rules for **tipping**. If you think you've received good service, particularly in restaurants or cafés, you may want to leave a tip of ten percent of the total bill (unless service has already been included). It's not normal, however, to leave tips in pubs, although bar staff are sometimes offered drinks, which they may accept in the form of money. The only other occasions when you'll be expected to tip are in hairdressers, taxis and smart hotels, where porters, bellboys and table waiters rely on being tipped to bump up their often-dismal wages.

Toilets

Finding a toilet in the remoter parts of Skye and the Western Isles can sometimes be tricky. The best bet is to stop in at a local café or pub, although they will almost always expect some form of custom in exchange for the use of their facilities.

Tourist information

The official tourist board is known as **VisitScotland** (www.visitscotland. com) and it runs **tourist offices** (often

---

Eating out price codes

Each **restaurant** and **café** reviewed in this Guide is accompanied by a price category, based on the cost of a **two-course meal** (or similar) for one, including a soft drink.

£	under £10
££	£11–£25
£££	£26–£40
££££	over £41

called iCentres) in virtually every major Scottish town. Opening hours are often fiendishly complex and often change at short notice. You'll find them at Portree and Stornoway in Skye and the Western Isles.

As well as being stacked full of souvenirs and other gifts, most iCs have on display a decent selection of leaflets, exhibits, maps and books relating to the local area. The staff are usually helpful and will do their best to help with enquiries, or even give you a hand booking accommodation, transport, attractions and restaurants. It's worth being aware that they're sometimes reluctant to divulge information about local attractions or accommodation options that aren't paid-up members of the tourist board, and a number of perfectly decent guesthouses and the like choose not to pay the fees.

Working in Scotland

All EU, Swiss nationals and EEA citizens can work in Scotland with a relevant visa. Other nationals need a **work permit** in order to work legally in the UK, with eligibility worked out on a points-based system. There are exceptions to the above rules, and these are constantly changing, so for the latest regulations visit http://gov.uk/government/organisations/uk-visas-and-immigration.

Festivals, events and spectator sports

There's a huge range of organized annual events on offer in Skye and the Western Isles, reflecting both vibrant contemporary culture and well-marketed heritage. Many tourists will home straight in on the Highland Games or music festivals, but there's more to the region, and to Scotland, than this: numerous regional celebrations perpetuate ancient customs. A few of the smaller, more obscure events, particularly those with a pagan bent, do not always welcome the casual visitor. The tourist board publishes a weighty list of all Scottish events on its website (www.visitscotland.com).

Hogmanay and Ne'er Day

Dec 31 and Jan 1
Traditionally more important to the Scots than Christmas, and known for the custom of "first-footing", when groups of revellers troop into neighbours' houses at midnight bearing gifts. More popular these days are huge and highly organized street parties in the larger towns.

Burns Night

Jan 25
Scots worldwide get stuck into haggis, whisky and vowel-grinding poetry to commemorate Scotland's greatest poet, Robert Burns.

Donald MacLeod Memorial Piping Competition

Early April, Stornoway
www.piobdm.com.
Some of the world's top bagpipers congregate every first Friday of April for this annual competition.

Highland Games

June
Beginning of the Highland Games season across the Highlands and Islands.

Fèis an Eilein (Skye Festival)

July, Skye
www.seall.co.uk.
Showcases Gaelic music and dancing at various locations across the island.

HebCelt

July, Stornoway
www.hebceltfest.com.
Four-day global Celtic music festival.

West Highland Yachting Week

Late July
www.whyw.co.uk.
A week of yacht racing and shore-based partying which moves en masse between Oban, Craobh and Tobermory.

The Isle of Skye Highland Games

August
www.skye-highland-games.co.uk.
A day testing the strength and endurance of participants, where Scots sign up for an array of traditional contests ranging from running to tossing the caber.

Skye Live

First weekend in Sept
www.skyelive.co.uk.
A riotous music festival in Skye featuring three jam-packed days of live music showcasing a wide range of genres from traditional Gaelic performances to DJ sets and electronic dance.

Chronology

c.4500 BC Neolithic people move into Scotland

c.2000 BC Callanish standing stones erected on Lewis in the Western Isles

100 BC–100 AD Fortified Iron Age brochs built across Scotland

43 AD Britain is invaded by the Romans

142 The Romans build the Antonine Wall between the Firth of Forth and the Firth of Clyde

410 The Romans withdraw from Britain

563 St Columba founds a monastery on Iona and begins to convert the Picts

795 Viking raids on the Scottish coast and islands begin

843 Kenneth MacAlpine becomes the first King of the Scots and the Picts

872 Orkney and Shetland come under Viking rule

1040 Macbeth is crowned the King of Scotland

1156 Somerled seizes the Kingdom of the Isles

1266 The Treaty of Perth hands the Hebrides back to Scotland from the Norwegians

1286 Death of Alexander III sparks the Wars of Scottish Independence

1314 Under Robert the Bruce, the Scots defeat the English at the Battle of Bannockburn

1320 The Declaration of Arbroath, asserting Scottish independence, is sent to the pope

1371 Robert II becomes the first of the Stewart (Stuart) kings to rule Scotland

1468 James III marries Margaret of Denmark and receives Orkney and Shetland as part of her dowry

1488 The Western Isles come under the rule of the Scottish Crown

1513 The Scots are defeated by the English at the Battle of Flodden Field

1560 The Scottish Church breaks with the Roman Catholic Church

1567 Abdication of Mary, Queen of Scots, and accession of James VI (aged 1)

1587 Mary, Queen of Scots, is executed on the orders of Queen Elizabeth I

1603 James VI of Scotland becomes James I of England

1638 National Covenant proclaimed by Scottish Presbyterians

1650 The Scots Royalist army is defeated at the Battle of Dunbar by the English under Oliver Cromwell

1689 Unsuccessful Jacobite uprising against William of Orange

1692 Glencoe massacre: 38 members of the MacDonald clan murdered by anti-Jacobite Campbells

1698 1200 Scots leave to establish a colony in Panama

1707 The Act of Union unites the kingdoms of Scotland and England

1715 Jacobite uprising against the accession of Hanoverian King George I

1746 Bonnie Prince Charlie's Jacobite army is defeated at the Battle of Culloden

1762 Beginning of the ruthless Highland Clearances

1843 The Great Disruption: a third of the Church of Scotland leave to form the Free Church of Scotland

1846 Highland potato famine: 1.7 million Scots emigrate

1886 Crofters' Holdings Act grants security of tenure in the Highlands and Islands

1914–18 100,000 Scots lose their lives in World War I

1919 208 soldiers returning from war die at sea when the Iolaire runs aground on rocks near Lewis

1928 The National Party of Scotland is formed

1939 The population of Scotland reaches five million

1939–45 34,000 Scottish soldiers lose their lives in World War II; 6000 civilians die in air raids

1979 Scottish referendum for devolution fails to gain the required forty percent

1996 The Stone of Scone is returned to Scotland

1999 Labour win the most seats in Scotland's first-ever general election

2009 Carol Ann Duffy becomes the first Scottish Poet Laureate

2011 The Scottish National Party win a majority in the Scottish Parliament

2013 Andy Murray becomes the first Scot to win Wimbledon men's singles title since 1896

2014 Scotland votes to remain part of the United Kingdom in an independence referendum

2016 Britain votes to leave the EU, although Scottish voters are primarily in favour of remaining, sparking disconnect within the UK

2019 Britain formally leaves the EU on 31 January

2023 Nicola Sturgeon resigns as first minister; former health secretary Humza Yousaf takes up the mantle, amid promises of leading Scotland to independence (despite the UK government refusing to consent to a second referendum)

Gaelic phrases, vocabulary and courses

One of the best introductory teach-yourself Gaelic courses is *Speaking Our Language* by Richard Cox, based on the TV series, much of which you can watch on YouTube. If you just want to get better at pronouncing Gaelic words, try *Blas na Gàidhlig* by Michael Bauer, or for a phrasebook, your best bet is *Everyday Gaelic* by Morag MacNeill. You can also do some self-learning on the Gaelic section of the BBC website www.bbc.co.uk.

Basic words and greetings

yes tha
no chan eil
hello hallo
how are you? ciamar a tha thu?
fine tha gu math
thank you tapadh leat
welcome fàilte
come in thig a-staigh
good day latha math
goodbye mar sin leat
good night oidhche mhath
who? cò?
where is...? càit a bheil...?
when? cuine?
what is it? dé tha ann?
morning madainn
evening feasgar
day là
night oidhche
tomorrow a-màireach
tonight a-nochd
cheers slàinte
yesterday an-dé
today an-diugh
tomorrow maireach

now a-nise
food lòn
bread aran
water uisge
milk bainne
beer leann
wine fion
whisky uisge beatha
Edinburgh Dun Eideann
Glasgow Glaschu
America Ameireaga
Ireland Eire
England Sasainn
London Lunnain

Some useful phrases

How much is that? Dè tha e 'cosg?
What's your name? Dè 'n t-ainm a th'ort?
Excuse me Gabh mo leisgeul
I'd like a double room 'Se rùm dùbailte tha mi'giarraigh
Do you speak Gaelic? A bheil Gàidhlig agad?
What is the Gaelic for ...? Dé a' Ghàidhlig a tha ... air?
I don't understand Chan eil mi 'tuigsinn
I don't know Chan eil fhios agam
It doesn't matter 'S coma
I'm sorry Tha mi duilich

Numbers and days

1 aon
2 dà/dhà
3 trì
4 ceithir
5 còig
6 sia
7 seachd

8 ochd	100 ceud
9 naoi	1000 mìle
10 deich	**Monday** Diluain
11 aon deug	**Tuesday** Dimàirt
20 fichead	**Wednesday** Diciadain
21 aon ar fhichead	**Thursday** Diardaoin
30 deug ar fhichead	**Friday** Dihaoine
40 dà fhichead	**Saturday** Disathurna
50 lethcheud	**Sunday** Didòmhnaich/La na Sàbaid
60 trì fichead	

Gaelic geographical and place-name terms

The purpose of the list below is to help with place-name derivations from Gaelic and with more detailed map-reading.

abhainn river

ach or auch, from achadh field

ail, aileach rock

Alba Scotland

aonach ridge

àird, ard, ardan or arden, from a point of land or height

aros dwelling

ault, from allt stream

bad brake or clump of trees

bagh bay

bal or bally, from baile town, village

balloch, from bealach mountain pass

ban white, fair

bàrr summit

beg, from beag small

ben, from beinn mountain

blair, from blàr field or battlefield

cairn, from càrn pile of stones

camas bay, harbour

cnoc hill

coll or colly, from coille wood or forest

corran a spit or point jutting into the sea

corrie, from coire round hollow in mountain-side, whirlpool

craig, from creag rock, crag

cruach bold hill

drum, from druim ridge

dubh black

dun or dum, from dùn for

eilean island

ess, from eas waterfall

fin, from fionn white

gair or gare, from geàrr short

garv, from garbh rough

geodha cove

glen, from gleann valley

gower or gour, goat from gabhar

inch, from innis meadow or island

inver, from inbhir river mouth

ken or kin, from ceann head

knock, from cnoc hill

kyle, from caolas narrow strait

lag hollow

larach site of an old ruin

liath grey

loch lake

meall round hill

mon, from monadh hill

more, from mór large, great

rannoch, from raineach bracken

ross, from ros promontory

rubha promontory

sgeir sea rock

sgurr sharp point

sron nose, prow or promontory

strath, from srath broad valley

tarbet, from tairbeart isthmus

tigh house

tir or tyre, from tìr land

torr hill, castle

tràigh shore

uig shelter

uisge water

SMALL PRINT

Publishing Information
Second Edition 2023

Distribution
UK, Ireland and Europe
Apa Publications (UK) Ltd; sales@roughguides.com
United States and Canada
Ingram Publisher Services; ips@ingramcontent.com
Australia and New Zealand
Booktopia; retailer@booktopia.com.au
Worldwide
Apa Publications (UK) Ltd; sales@roughguides.com
Special Sales, Content Licensing and CoPublishing
Rough Guides can be purchased in bulk quantities at discounted prices. We can create special editions, personalised jackets and corporate imprints tailored to your needs. sales@roughguides.com.
roughguides.com
Printed in China

This book was produced using **Typefi** automated publishing software.

Rough Guide Credits
Editor: Annie Warren
Cartography: Katie Bennett
Picture editor: Tom Smyth
Layout: Pradeep Thapliyal
Original design: Richard Czapnik
Head of DTP and Pre-Press: Rebeka Davies
Head of Publishing: Sarah Clark

Acknowledgements
Thank you to Kathryn at the *Uist Forest Retreat* for all your local knowledge and insights, Carla Regler for your photography tips, and the team at the Eriskay Pony Society for your diligence in explaining the island's magnificent native beasts. A big thank you to editing whizz Annie for whipping my notes into shape.

SMALL PRINT

About the author

Joanna Reeves is a Sussex-based travel writer and editor for whom Skye and the Outer Hebrides hold a special place in her heart – she even got engaged at a remote lochside cabin in South Uist. She was the editor of the *Rough Guide to the 100 Best Places in Scotland*.

Help us update

We've gone to a lot of effort to ensure that this edition of the **Pocket Rough Guide Isle of Skye and the Western Isles** is accurate and up-to-date. However, things change – places get "discovered", opening hours are notoriously fickle, restaurants and rooms raise prices or lower standards. If you feel we've got it wrong or left something out, we'd like to know, and if you can remember the address, the price, the hours, the phone number, so much the better.

Please send your comments with the subject line "**Pocket Rough Guide Isle of Skye and the Western Isles Update**" to mail@uk.roughguides.com. We'll credit all contributions and send a copy of the next edition (or any other Rough Guide if you prefer) for the very best emails.

Photo Credits

(Key: T-top; C-centre; B-bottom; L-left; R-right)

Alamy 10, 12/13T, 12/13B, 14T, 15B, 16B, 17B, 17T, 22/23, 34, 46, 47, 49, 83
Alan Donaldson/Kinloch Lodge 48
Getty Images 15T, 53, 54
iStock 11T, 11B, 12L, 27, 60, 65
Kenny Lam/VisitScotland 6, 58, 74
Paul Tomkins/VisitScotland 2T, 4, 13C, 21C, 59T, 70, 90, 93, 94, 95, 96, 98, 99, 101, 102/103, 110/111

Shutterstock 1, 2BL, 2C, 2BR, 5, 14B, 16T, 18T, 18C, 18B, 19T, 19C, 19B, 20T, 20C, 20B, 21T, 21B, 24, 28, 30, 33, 35, 37, 39, 40, 41, 42, 44, 45, 50, 51, 56, 57, 59B, 63, 66, 67, 69, 71, 72, 73, 75, 76, 77, 80, 81, 84, 85, 87, 88, 97, 100

Cover: Portree **Aeypix/Shutterstock**

Index

NOTES

NOTES